# ART
# LONDON

# ART
# LONDON

## A GUIDE TO PLACES, ARTISTS AND EVENTS

Hettie Judah

Photographs by Alex Schneideman

ACC ART BOOKS

# INTRODUCTION

London today is a booming art city. Its colleges are cosmopolitan, its blockbuster exhibitions booked up months in advance, and its major fairs and auctions comfortably lodged in collectors' calendars. In this city, art can be discovered in every setting; from artist-run spaces in Deptford to the slickest galleries in Mayfair; from scrappy student pop-ups to crowning retrospectives at the Royal Academy.

It was not always thus: had this book been written forty years earlier, it would have been a far slimmer volume. In 1978, the ICA held a conference on 'The State of British Art', in which crisis was the dominant mood. The venerable art magazine *Studio International* suspended publishing. For European collectors London was not even an intriguing stopover en route to New York. In the British press, works of contemporary art were approached as if an endless series of bad jokes. The idea that some two decades on, Tate Modern would draw five million visitors in its first year – and would continue expanding to accommodate ever growing crowds – was unthinkable.

That was not the city's first creative crisis. Its art scene has ebbed and flowed like the waters of the Thames. Like the Thames, too, it has borne abundant love and conflict, junk, folly and sewage. Today home to some of the world's greatest museums, London for centuries operated in the shadow of Florence, Venice and Genoa, Antwerp and Amsterdam, Paris, Berlin and New York.

Nevertheless, the city has proved a magnet for talent: surprisingly few of London's great artists were born here.

There is no single art history of London. It is a suite of parallel stories rather than a grand overarching narrative. The piecemeal, neighbourhood-by-neighbourhood structure of this book reflects a patchwork of activity: Flemish artists at the Tudor court; connoisseurs of Covent Garden's taverns and brothels in the eighteenth century; the Pre-Raphaelite Brotherhood; the Whitechapel Boys (and girls) from Jewish immigrant communities in the East End; the Black Arts Movement of the 1980s. Here, too, are isolated figures, among them artist-visionary William Blake and living sculptures Gilbert & George.

In 1998 London's great artworld diarist Louisa Buck published the primer *Moving Targets*. Over twenty years on, her choice of title is more apposite than ever: London's artworld was and is impossible to pin down. Galleries open and close overnight, districts heat up and cool down again as fast as opportunistic landlords rocket the rent. Whole ecosystems are wiped out as studio complexes are sold for development. Ironically, nostalgia often flares for the crisis years of the 1970s, when London's abandoned buildings offered space to live, work and show, safely hidden from the international market.

London can be fast-paced, brutal and demanding: many artists have moved to Berlin, Lisbon, Athens, and England's South East. Yet the city lacks neither artists nor galleries; if anything, the sheer volume of art can feel overwhelming. Perhaps some kind of guide to art in London, past and present, might come in handy?

## A NOTE ON STRUCTURE

*Art London* is organised by loosely defined districts. Within them, sites are designated 'institutions' or 'commercial galleries'. For the purposes of this book, 'institution' indicates a venue not funded primarily by sales, be that an artist-run space, private foundation or major museum. As with the boundaries of London's neighbourhoods, these designations are approximate.

The information on venues is interspersed with narrative texts on places, movements and artists through the ages, along with profiles of some of London's leading contemporary practitioners.

# BUYING ART

However coy they may appear, all the commercial galleries listed in Art London do actually sell work, though to whom and at what price are closely guarded secrets. Let the gallery's location and ambiance be your guide; if you love something, and think it might be within range, there's no harm in asking the gallerist about it. Works in artist-run and studio spaces may well also be for sale; again, no harm in asking. London has a packed schedule of fairs selling art, high-end craft and design; some deliberately positioned at the affordable end, others very much not (see overleaf for a list of London's art fairs). If you have lofty tastes not met by your limited budget, editions (often prints, photographic or otherwise) are a more accessible entry point. Camden Arts Centre, Chisenhale, ICA, South London Gallery, Studio Voltaire, Serpentine and Whitechapel all invite their exhibiting artists to create editions to help raise funds for the gallery; be warned, prices go up as the edition progressively sells out. Studio Voltaire's House of Voltaire features wildly fashionable artist collabs ranging from tea towels and t-shirts to ceramics and knitwear. Look out, too, for fund-raising initiatives like Drawing Room's biannual auction of works on paper donated by some of Britain's most prominent artists.

# FAIRS AND FIXTURES

## JANUARY

### Condo

*Citywide*

Cooperative scheme bringing independent galleries from around the world to London to share exhibition space with local outfits spread around the city. The party atmosphere of the opening weekend makes it a popular fixture.

**condocomplex.org**

### London Art Fair

*Islington Design Centre, 52 Upper Street, Angel N1 0QH*

Long-established fair with a more British flavour, showing modern and contemporary work.

**londonartfair.co.uk**

## MARCH

### The Other Art Fair

*Truman Brewery, Brick Lane, E1 6QR*

Art sold directly by artists, no galleries involved.

**Theotherartfair.com**

### Affordable Art Fair Battersea

*Battersea Evolution, Battersea Park, SW11 4NJ*

Galleries from around the world selling accessibly priced artworks.

**Affordableartfair.com**

## APRIL

### London Original Print Fair

*Royal Academy of Arts, Burlington House, Piccadilly, W1J 0BD*

Long-established editions fair.

**Londonoriginalprintfair.com**

## MAY

### Affordable Art Fair Hampstead

*Lower Fairground Site, East Heath Road, Hampstead Heath, NW3 1TH*

Hampstead edition of the fair that sells accessibly priced artworks from galleries around the world.

**Affordableartfair.com**

### Draw Art Fair

*Saatchi Gallery, Duke of York's Headquarters, King's Road, Chelsea, SW3 4RY*

Art fair specialising in drawing.

**Drawartfair.com**

### Photo London

*Somerset House, Strand, WC2R 1LA*

Specialist photography fair accompanied by a broad program of exhibitions, talks and events.

**Photolondon.org**

### Block Universe

*Citywide*

Unmissable performance art festival.

**Blockuniverse.co.uk**

## JUNE

### Art school graduation shows

*Various locations*

### Royal Academy Summer Exhibition

*Royal Academy of Arts, Burlington House, Piccadilly, W1J 0BD*

The world's largest open-submission art show, in operation since 1769.

**Royalacademy.org.uk**

### Mayfair Art Weekend

*Various locations in Mayfair*

Weekend celebration led by commercial galleries in Mayfair and St James's. Talks, tours and special events.

**Mayfairartweekend.com**

### Masterpiece

*Grounds of The Royal Hospital, Chelsea, SW3 4LW*

High-end art, design, furniture and jewellery.

**Masterpiecefair.com**

### The Art Car Boot Fair

*Cubitt Square, Stable Street, King's Cross, N1C 4BT*

Informal outdoor market where artists (many eminent) flog specially made, accessibly priced works from car boot pitches.

**Artcarbootfair.com**

# JULY

## Art Night

*Various locations*
Riotous night-long festival of art commissions and performances occupying a different district of the city every year.
**artnight.london**

## The Other Art Fair, King's Cross

*West Handyside Canopy, 1 Wharf Road, King's Cross, N1C 4BZ*
More art sold directly by artists, no galleries involved; this time in King's Cross.
**theotherartfair.com**

# SEPTEMBER

## START Art Fair

*Saatchi Gallery, Duke of York's Headquarters, King's Road, Chelsea, SW3 4RY*
Art with a more international edge.
**startartfair.com**

# OCTOBER

## PAD London

*Berkeley Square, W1*
Aka The Pavilion of Art and Design; a fair of high-end decorative arts.
**pad-fairs.com/london**

## Frieze London

*Regents Park, NW1 4HA*
Top-end contemporary art fair.
**frieze.com/fairs/frieze-london**

## Frieze Masters

*Regent's Park, NW1 4HA*
Works made before 2000.
**frieze.com/fairs/frieze-masters**

## 1–54 Contemporary African Art Fair

*Somerset House, Strand, WC2R 1LA*
Collection of international galleries showing work from established and emerging artists.
**1-54.com/london**

## Affordable Art Fair Battersea

*Battersea Evolution, Battersea Park, SW11 4NJ*
Autumn incarnation of the fair, selling accessibly priced artworks.
**affordableartfair.com**

## The Other Art Fair

*Victoria House, Southampton Row, WC1B 5HR*
Art sold directly by artists, no galleries involved; this time in Holborn.
**theotherartfair.com**

# MAYFAIR

# INSTITUTIONS

**MIMOSA HOUSE**
12 Princes Street, W1B 2LL
mimosahouse.co.uk

A non-profit hyper sensitised to current arguments and preoccupations within the international scene. The small upstairs spaces house themed shows of work by women and queer artists from across the generations. Free.

**ROYAL ACADEMY OF ARTS**
Burlington House, Piccadilly, W1J 0BD
AND
6 Burlington Gardens, W1S 3ET
royalacademy.org.uk

Eminent hybrid institution housing heavyweight temporary exhibitions, an elite postgraduate art school and the headquarters of an elect body of artists and architects known as Royal Academicians. Exhibitions ticketed.

Royal Academy of Arts; Phyllida Barlow, *cul-de-sac* (2019)
(Previous pages: Royal Academy of Arts, Annenberg Courtyard)

# WOMEN AT THE ROYAL ACADEMY

There were two women among the 34 founders of the Royal Academy of Arts in 1768. Mary Moser and Angelica Kauffman were also the last women to be nominated RA until Dame Laura Knight in 1936. At the Academy Schools, the first female student – Laura Herford – was admitted by accident in 1860 after submitting work signed with initials. Subsequent female students were banned from life class, with a concession to study the partially draped figure made in the 1890s. Even in the 1960s, the three female academicians invited to vote for a new president were barred from a dinner that followed. 'This is an ignominious situation which…I will not lend myself to ever again,' Gertrude Hermes wrote in a spirited complaint. 'It was humiliating and I left hurriedly.' The gender balance is shifting, if slowly. Today, around a third of Academicians are women. Does it matter? Yes, argues Sonia Boyce, the first Black woman elected RA: 'The most important thing is that one's voted in by one's peers. As an institution, the Royal Academy is there to foster what is emerging as well as what is established; within that context the work of women artists and Black artists has to be thought about.'

# THE SUMMER EXHIBITION

Once known simply as 'The Exhibition', the Royal Academy's grand display – historically, the centrepiece of London's art calendar – has been held annually since 1769. Works by Royal Academicians, and thousands of others selected by a committee from open submissions, hang side by side (and, in the early years, frame to frame, floor to ceiling). Works are for sale, with the Academy's cut helping fund their Schools. The politics of which works are selected, and also where and how they are hung, was once a subject of much competition. Before the paintings were arranged, a strip of wooden beading was placed along the wall two or three feet above head height. The paintings considered most important – usually history paintings and portraits – were placed 'on the line', and all other works arranged around them. The question of which paintings were chosen for display on the line thus became tantamount to a judgement of merit. Thomas Gainsborough – a founding academician, and great rival to Sir Joshua Reynolds – removed all his paintings from the 1784 exhibition after the committee refused to hang one of his royal portraits in a lower position that would break the line.

# SIR JOSHUA REYNOLDS

The first president of the Royal Academy was the eighteenth century's leading portrait painter. Born in Devon, after a period of apprenticeship he travelled widely in southern Europe in his twenties, and spent two years in Rome studying the Old Masters. He formed an association with the younger Italian artist Giuseppe Marchi, who accompanied him on his return to England, eventually becoming his studio assistant when Reynolds settled in London in 1753. Reynolds was prolific – his rapid production achieved with the assistance of Marchi or one of his pupils, who painted the sitters' clothing. In 1764, Reynolds formed a dining club known simply as 'The Club' with essayist Samuel Johnson and philosopher Edmund Burke. The Club met weekly, on Monday nights, at the Turks Head at 9 Gerrard Street in Soho. Reynolds set out his theories on art in a series of lectures delivered to the Academy and published as *Discourses on Art*. Painted in his idealised 'Grand Manner', Reynolds's portraits have aged poorly, the red and flesh tones faded and the bitumen blacks cracked and flattened.

# THE INTERNATIONAL SURREALIST EXHIBITION

Boiled string, a diving suit, kippers and a rotting pork chop all made appearances at the Surrealists' show at the New Burlington Galleries in 1936. Among the European artists invited were Pablo Picasso, René Magritte, Max Ernst, Alexander Calder, Giorgio de Chirico, Marcel Duchamp, Alberto Giacometti, Paul Klee, Joan Miró, Meret Oppenheim, Man Ray and Salvador Dalí. The initiative of artists Roland Penrose and Paul Nash, and art critic Herbert Read, it offered British audiences the first sight of a cultural movement causing a sensation on the other side of the Channel and already influencing art on these shores. And cause a sensation it did: 23,000 came to see the exhibition. The opening events stopped traffic, as Dalí performed bolted inside in a diving suit, nearly suffocating in the process. Painter Sheila Legge appeared carrying a pork chop, her head masked in rose petals and ladybirds, while poet Dylan Thomas offered visitors cups of string. In his exhibition text, Herbert Read counselled visitors to look beyond the absurdity. 'It is not just another amusing stunt. It is defiant – the desperate act of men too profoundly convinced of the rottenness of our civilisation to want to save a shred of its respectability.'

# KITCHEN SINK SCHOOL

Mayfair seems an unlikely point of origin for a movement given to unvarnished depiction of domestic life, but it is here, at the Beaux Art Gallery, that four Royal College of Art graduates were shown in succession between 1952-54. John Bratby, Jack Smith, Derrick Greaves and Edward Middleditch were known as the Beaux Arts Quartet until critic David Sylvester penned a critical essay on these 'young painters of the kitchen-sink school' for *Encounter* magazine in 1954, and the name stuck. 'The post-war generation takes us back from the studio to the kitchen. Dead ducks, rabbits and fish – especially skate – can be found there, as in the expressionist slaughterhouse, but only as part of an inventory which includes every kind of food and drink, every kind of utensil and implement, the usual plain furniture, and even the baby's nappies on the line. Everything but the kitchen sink? The kitchen sink too.' Sylvester's misgivings notwithstanding, the quartet represented Britain at the Venice Biennale in 1956. The term 'Kitchen sink' captured the era's social restlessness, and the term was adopted to describe the disillusioned realism of British New Wave cinema and radical works for theatre such as John Osborne's *Look Back in Anger*.

# AESTHETIC MOVEMENT

A commitment to art for art's sake, and the pursuit of beauty, craftsmanship and self-expression: Aestheticism was a riposte to the fussy repressiveness of Victorian Britain and industrial production. This call to sensual beauty drew James Abbott McNeill Whistler, G.F. Watts, Edward Burne-Jones, Frederic, Lord Leighton and Lawrence Alma-Tadema, who showed at Bond Street's Grosvenor Gallery. Reviewing the opening exhibition in 1877, John Ruskin was scathing in his assessment of Whistler's *Nocturne in Black and Gold (The Falling Rocket)*: 'I have seen, and heard, much of Cockney impudence before now; but never expected to hear a coxcomb ask two hundred guineas for flinging a pot of paint in the public's face.' The artist sued, winning the landmark case, but bankrupting himself in the process. The Grosvenor distanced itself from the Royal Academy in its exhibition designs: pictures were widely spaced on scarlet silk damask. It also showed works by women, among them Laura Alma-Tadema, Marianne Stokes and Annie Swynnerton. Within the literary world, the movement reaches its epitome in the life and work of Oscar Wilde. The grotesque spectacle of his arrest, trial and imprisonment did for the Aesthetic Movement as surely as it did for poor Wilde.

# COMMERCIAL GALLERIES

## ALMINE RECH
Grosvenor Hill, Broadbent House,
W1K 3JH
alminerech.com

Slick London outpost for the elegant Parisian gallerist with spaces, too, in Brussels and New York. Stars of the stable include Taryn Simon, Jeff Koons and James Turrell.

## ANNELY JUDA
Fourth Floor, 23 Dering Street,
W1S 1AW
annelyjudafineart.co.uk

A fixture on London's scene since 1960, Annely Juda shows contemporary artists as well as figures from the twentieth-century avant-garde: Naum Gabo, Kazimir Malevich, László Moholy-Nagy, Ben Nicholson, Alexander Rodchenko and Kurt Schwitters.

## BEAUX ARTS
48 Maddox Street, W1S 1AY
beauxartslondon.uk

Other galleries may be eyeing out-of-town spaces; Beaux Arts moved in the other direction, opening first in St Ives in the 1970s. Cornwall is still present in the work of Barbara Hepworth, Patrick Heron, Roger Hilton and Terry Frost, shown alongside contemporary artists including Nick Hornby and Chris Stevens.

## BELMACZ
45 Davies Street, W1K 4LX
belmacz.com

Jeweller and gallerist Julia Muggenburg has an eye for arresting affinities. Here she presides over a space of appropriately jewel-box dimensions, hosting boldly conceptual group shows alongside gems of her own, striking design.

## BEN BROWN FINE ARTS
12 Brook's Mews, W1K 4DG
benbrownfinearts.com

Working in the contemporary art department at Sotheby's, Ben Brown acquired an interest in twentieth-century Italian art. He opened his Italo-centric gallery in 2004, showing work by Alighiero Boetti and Lucio Fontana as well as that of distinctly non-Italian artists Vik Muniz, Gavin Turk, Not Vital and designer Ron Arad, among others.

## BLAIN/SOUTHERN
4 Hanover Square, W1S 1BP
blainsouthern.com

Blain/Southern broadcast their audacious approach through a big, glass-fronted corner gallery prominently positioned opposite Vogue House. A muscular list includes Sean Scully, Bill Viola, Rachel Howard and Tim Noble & Sue Webster. There are brains here as well as brawn: thoughtful thematic shows, and guest spots for emerging artists.

## CARDI GALLERY
22 Grafton Street, W1S 4EX
cardigallery.com

Italian gallery showing Arte Povera, Zero Group and the work of associated post-war European artists from a magnificent townhouse gallery.

## CARL KOSTYÁL
12a Savile Row, W1S 3PQ
kostyal.com

Kostyál is a collector and dealer; in other words he shows whatever he likes, on Savile Row and in Stockholm, but doesn't represent artists. On current evidence, what he likes is exciting: Mandy El-Sayegh, Sara Cwynar, Petra Cortright, as well as less-shown senior figures.

## DAVID GILL
2-4 King Street, SW1Y 6QP
davidgillgallery.com

As a term, 'design art' sounds rather 2008; no matter, this crossover territory has been Gill's stamping ground for

Blain/Southern, Mayfair

decades. The gallery is home to arty-minded designers, among them Fredrikson Stallard and the Campana Brothers, and design-minded artists such as Michele Oka Doner and ceramicist Lena Peters.

## DAVID ZWIRNER
24 Grafton Street, W1S 4EZ
davidzwirner.com

London digs for the powerhouse New York gallery, showing works over two floors. Strong on contemporary painting, with an international roster that includes Tomma Abts, Rose Wylie, Kerry James Marshall, Lisa Yuskavage and Luc Tuymans.

## FLOWERS GALLERY
21 Cork Street, W1S 3LZ
AND
82 Kingsland Road, E2 8DP
flowersgallery.com

Angela Flowers founded her London gallery in 1970, and was in the first wave to open in the East End in the 1980s during the BritArt blossoming. Flowers represents a diverse list, in which eminent photographers (Edward Burtynsky, Nadav Kander…) sit alongside New Glasgow Boys Peter Howson and Ken Currie, and fleshy, detailed, unflinching portraits by Ishbel Myerscough.

## GAGOSIAN GROSVENOR HILL
20 Grosvenor Hill, W1K 3QD
gagosian.com

The fanciest of Gagosian's three London spaces, this Caruso St John-designed gallery houses the creamiest of this very creamy gallery's offering. Testosterone-laden solo shows to date include Cy Twombly, Ed Ruscha, Picasso, Richard Serra and Brice Marden. Around the corner, the small Gagosian Davies Street deploys a storefront location to eye-catching effect.

## GALERIE MAX HETZLER
41 Dover Street, W1S 4NS
maxhetzler.com

A small London outpost for the influential German gallerist known for championing a maverick generation of German artists emerging in the early 1980s, among them Günther Förg, Martin Kippenberger and Albert Oehlen. Ties to the UK and US have seen the gallery's interests broaden.

## GALERIE THADDAEUS ROPAC
Ely House, 37 Dover Street, W1S 4NJ
ropac.net

Occupying a grand townhouse built for the Bishop of Ely in the 1770s, Austrian gallerist Thaddaeus Ropac has the most beautiful gallery in London. All that stately glamour is just set dressing for the art – shows by big beasts including

Georg Baselitz, Anselm Kiefer and Tony Cragg, as well as younger talents such as Oliver Beer, Cory Arcangel and Alvaro Barrington.

## HAMILTONS
13 Carlos Place, W1K 2EU
hamiltonsgallery.com

One of London's leading photographic galleries, Hamiltons occupies an extraordinary building – an old racquets court and music room belonging to the Courtauld family. The short list of artists represented is all killer (also all male – which perhaps speaks more about the photographic sphere than it does the gallery), including Daido Moriyama, Helmut Newton, Irving Penn, Don McCullin and Nobuyoshi Araki.

## HAUSER & WIRTH SAVILE ROW
23 Savile Row, W1S 2ET
hauserwirth.com

Gallerists, publishers, educators, farmers, gardeners, restaurateurs and now hoteliers: Swiss art juggernaut Hauser & Wirth has transformed the role and position of the commercial gallery over the last decade. It's no longer just about selling art – it's about creating the universe in which to position it. Two adjacent high-ceilinged galleries show work by a thoughtful and surprising contemporary and modern roster, including Roni Horn, Louise Bourgeois, Lorna Simpson and Pierre Huyghe.

## HUXLEY-PARLOUR
3-5 Swallow Street, W1B 4DE
huxleyparlour.com

In a previous pre-Parlour incarnation this gallery specialised in modern and contemporary photography. They still show ace snappers, among them Alec Soth, Edward Weston, Berenice Abbott, Bill Brandt and Vivian Maier. As Huxley-Parlour, they've widened their interest to other media; don't faint if you turn up and they have a painting show on.

## KAMEL MENNOUR
51 Brook Street, W1K 4HR
kamelmennour.com

A diminutive space tucked into the façade of Claridge's Hotel. Don't let the size fool you: on the other side of the Channel, Kamel Mennour is a force to be reckoned with, and the artists the gallery works with include many of the most exciting figures of the moment: Mohamed Bourouissa, Petrit Halilaj, Alicja Kwade and Camille Henrot.

Gagosian Grosvenor Hill, Mayfair

Hauser & Wirth, Mayfair

Galerie Thaddaeus Ropac, Mayfair; Erwin Wurm exhibition

## LAZINC
29 Sackville Street, W1S 3DX
lazinc.com

In the world of street art (and street-adjacent art) Steve Lazarides has walked the walk, working with Banksy for 11 years, and becoming his de facto agent in the process. He's one of the few the notoriously camera-shy art prankster trusts to handle his work, though these days he has to share Lazarides with his muralist brethren, among them JR, eL Seed, Invader and Mode 2.

## LÉVY GORVY
22 Old Bond Street, W1S 4PY
levygorvy.com

Plush surroundings above London's prime luxury goods strip give this gallery specialising in twentieth-century art an aura of old money, like walking into a private apartment. Founded by art adviser Dominique Lévy, and Brett Gorvy, formerly chairman of Christie's, Lévy Gorvy has positioned itself as a heavyweight. Expect big names, collectible furniture and slick concepts.

## LUXEMBOURG AND DAYAN
2 Savile Row, W1S 3PA
luxembourgdayan.com

L&D's thing is post-war European art – Alighiero Boetti, Alberto Burri, Alberto Giacometti, César and their ilk – which they show solo and in group shows with contemporary works from a dude-heavy list.

## LYNDSEY INGRAM
20 Bourdon Street, W1K 3PL
lyndseyingram.com

Prints, editions, and works on paper from a lovely list of artists, ranging from Ed Ruscha and Kiki Smith through to Bridget Riley, Grayson Perry and David Shrigley.

## MADDOX ART
9 Maddox Street, W1S 2QE
AND
112 Westbourne Grove, W2 5RU
AND
8 Shepherd Street, W1J 7JE
maddoxgallery.com

With two galleries in Mayfair, and others in Notting Hill, Gstaad and Los Angeles, Maddox certainly know how to put themselves where the money is. They also know how to put themselves in the limelight, with curator/director James Nicholls a keen presence on camera. What's on the walls? For the most part, a lightweight mix of street art and latter-day pop.

## MARLBOROUGH FINE ART
6 Albemarle Street, W1S 4BY
marlboroughlondon.com

Founded after the Second World War, Marlborough has history, starting with shows by Degas, van Gogh, Monet, Renoir and their contemporaries, before developing important relationships with London artists, among them

Francis Bacon, Lynn Chadwick, Barbara Hepworth, Henry Moore and Ben Nicholson. The gallery continues to show new works by painters Paula Rego, Frank Auerbach and Maggi Hambling.

**MASSIMO DE CARLO**
55 South Audley Street, W1K 2QH
massimodecarlo.com

A dash of Milano cool in London. Massimo de Carlo has worked with Italy's prime art provocateur Maurizio Cattelan since the 1980s. Retaining an irreverent edge, today the stable is a mix of European, North American and Chinese artists – think Andra Ursuta, Carsten Höller, Gelitin, Yan Pei-Ming – reflecting the distribution of its galleries.

**MAZZOLENI**
27 Albemarle Street, W1S 4HZ,
mazzoleniart.com

Venerable Turin gallery (the space back home is a three-storey *palazzo*) largely showing twentieth-century Italian art.

# CORK STREET

From the 1920s to the 1990s, Cork Street was the epicentre of London's contemporary scene. Fred Mayor opened the Mayor Gallery in 1925 – still on Cork Street today, in a first floor space – showing works by the European avant-garde. In 1933, the gallery also became the headquarters of the short-lived Unit One group founded by Paul Nash. In 1936, Redfern Gallery moved to its current address at 20 Cork Street, and in 1938 Peggy Guggenheim opened her gallery Guggenheim Jeune – with artist Marcel Duchamp as advisor – in an upstairs space at number 30. Kicking off with controversial works by Jean Cocteau, Guggenheim Jeune also staged the first London exhibition by Wassily Kandinsky, before closing as war broke out the following year. The Redfern and Mayor galleries re-opened in the years after the war, followed by others, among them Victor Waddington, in 1957, and his son Leslie, who opened his own gallery at number 11 in 1966. Leslie Waddington's gallery championed abstract art, and, in the 1980s, Georg Baselitz, Barry Flanagan and Michael Craig-Martin. The fortunes of Cork Street wax and wane with rising rates and changing fashions; Mayfair and St James's remain important, but it is hard for small independent galleries to compete.

## MICHAEL WERNER
22 Upper Brook Street, W1K 7PZ
michaelwerner.com

With roots in 1960s Berlin, Michael Werner's gallery goes big on late twentieth-century European art – Per Kirkeby, Sigmar Polke, James Lee Byars and, more recently, Kai Althoff, Peter Doig and Hurvin Anderson – reflecting connections and relationships dating back decades. Tucked away in a curlicued townhouse, the London gallery is junior sibling to a grander concern in New York and storied spaces in Germany.

## NAHMAD PROJECTS
2 Cork Street, W1S 3LB
nahmadprojects.com

The name, in art circles, is legendary – the Nahmad family is one of the world's great dealerships – but this gallery, run by the younger Joseph Nahmad, breaks from the family's traditional preference for modern masters to sample more experimental contemporary fare, bringing you Petra Cortright and Alexander Calder both.

## OLIVIER MALINGUE
First Floor
143 New Bond Street, W1S 2TP
oliviermalingue.com

Olivier earned his artworld stripes working alongside his father Daniel at the venerable Malingue gallery in Paris. His brother Edouard went on to found a gallery in Hong Kong, and Olivier in London. The menu is modern European masters with a smattering of star turns from East Asia.

## ORDOVAS
25 Savile Row, W1S 2ER
ordovasart.com

Dealership with substantial premises showing three blue-chip shows a year under the direction of Pilar Ordovas (ex-Christie's, ex-Gagosian).

## PACE
6 Burlington Gardens, W1S 3ET
pacegallery.com

A global force: with ten galleries including outposts in Palo Alto, Seoul and Geneva, Pace means business. The location of this London gallery – nestled into the grand back end of the Royal Academy – hints at the image it's broadcasting. Slick shows from a list of artists that would stretch from the gallery doormat to Piccadilly Circus, from Vito Acconci to Zhang Xiaogang.

## PARAFIN
18 Woodstock Street, W1C 2AL
parafin.co.uk

Young gallery showing interesting works by emerging and mid-career artists. Among them, Alison Watt's cool white paintings of drapery, and high-concept video and photographic installations by Melanie Manchot.

# GROOVY BOB

Robert Fraser – aka Groovy Bob – opened his gallery on Duke Street in 1962, bringing the full swing of swinging London into Mayfair. Artists, writers and actors crossed paths with The Beatles and The Rolling Stones at Fraser's gallery, and his flat on Mount Street. The photograph of him handcuffed to Mick Jagger after the notorious Redlands drugs bust was immortalised by Richard Hamilton in the print series *Swingeing London*. As a gallerist, Fraser had passion and knowledge, but lacked patience and business sense. Despite a starry exhibition roster and even starrier clientele, the gallery racked up debts and closed in 1969.

# THE CAVE OF THE GOLDEN CALF

It was not hard to find the subterranean cabaret theatre at 9 Heddon Street – a relief by Eric Gill outside showed a golden calf with prominent genitalia, flanked by flaccid penises. Opened by Frida Strindberg – ex wife of August Strindberg – on 26 June 1912, the Cave was a labour of love, not least for the artists who contributed to its decadent, suggestive interiors and who, it seems, were never paid. Spencer Gore directed proceedings. Beside his own large murals – including a hunting scene with tigers, indebted to Gauguin's paintings of Tahiti – he commissioned three large murals by Charles Ginner. Wyndham Lewis painted a drop curtain to resemble raw meat, and Eric Gill's aroused calf reappeared as a sculpture in the foyer. Named for the idol worshipped by the Israelites as Moses ascended Mount Sinai, such was the Cave's reputation for orgiastic dissolution that it was cited in a sensational divorce case in 1914. By then the club was entering its swansong. Strindberg – memorably described by Augustus John as 'the walking hell-bitch of the Western World' – was in difficulties. She closed the club that year, leaving for the United States and apparently taking all the artworks with her.

## PIPPY HOULDSWORTH
6 Heddon Street, W1B 4BT
houldsworth.co.uk

A gallery not averse to strong political work from across the generations; artists include taboo-busting feminist Mary Kelly and rebel New York collective The Bruce High Quality Foundation. Passions are pursued through special projects and small displays in a glass-fronted niche aka The Box.

## RICHARD SALTOUN
41 Dover Street, W1S 4NS
richardsaltoun.com

On a mission to keep under-valued feminist and conceptual artists in the public eye, Richard Saltoun work with figures beloved of artists and art students, but perhaps less represented in public collections. Increased public visibility of work by photographer Jo Spence, surreal collagist Penny Slinger, and performance artist Rose English is due in part to this gallery's shows and scholarship.

## ROBILANT + VOENA
38 Dover Street, W1S 4NL
robilantvoena.com

Italian gallery with one eye on the Old Masters and the other on post-war Italian art.

## SADIE COLES HQ DAVIES STREET
1 Davies Street, W1K 3DB
AND
62 Kingly Street, W1B 5QN
sadiecoles.com

A secondary shopfront space used to interesting public effect by Sadie Coles HQ, one of London's most consistently stimulating contemporary galleries.

## SIMON LEE
12 Berkeley Street, W1J 8DT
simonleegallery.com

Over nearly two decades in Mayfair, Simon Lee have built up relationships with contemporary artists working across all media, from painters Clare Woods and George Condo to textile-centric assemblage artist Eric N. Mack and photographer and film maker Larry Clark.

## SPRÜTH MAGERS
7A Grafton Street, W1S 4EJ
spruethmagers.com

Born out of Cologne's booming contemporary art scene in the 1980s, Sprüth Magers is now an international presence. With outposts in London, LA, Berlin and Hong Kong, Philomene Magers and Monika Sprüth have maintained important links to the artists – many female – that they championed back in the day, among them Rosemarie Trockel, Fischli & Weiss, Jenny Holzer, Barbara Kruger and Cindy Sherman.

## STEPHEN FRIEDMAN
25-28 Old Burlington Street, W1S 3AN
stephenfriedman.com

Stephen Friedman is driven by passion. Among the Brits are Yinka Shonibare CBE and David Shrigley; from Europe, Thomas Hirschhorn and Mamma Andersson; from the US, Rivane Neuenschwander and Melvin Edwards. Consistently interesting shows across two galleries.

## TIMOTHY TAYLOR
timothytaylor.com
New venue to be confirmed

Well-connected London dealer representing a very mixed list, including virtual reality pioneer and film-maker Shezad Dawood, School of London veterans Frank Auerbach and Leon Kossoff, and fabulous mystic feminist Kiki Smith.

## VICTORIA MIRO
14 St George Street, W1S 1FE
victoria-miro.com

This long-established and highly respected gallery has two London sites – a modest space on a prime spot in Mayfair, and a sprawling three-storey space in Islington. There are plenty of powerful female artists scattered across the 40-strong list, among them Yayoi Kusama, Chantal Joffe, Njideka Akunyili Crosby and Sarah Sze.

Sprüth Magers Gallery, Mayfair

# EILEEN AGAR AND
# *ANGEL OF ANARCHY*

'I hope to die in a sparkling moment' concluded Eileen Agar's autobiography, following a life full of them. Agar discovered art at secondary school in Kent during the First World War. After studying at the Slade School, she moved to Paris where she fell in with surrealists André Breton and Paul Éluard. Breton's *Surrealist Manifesto* inspired a new direction: collage, photography and sculpture from found objects. Agar's work was included in the International Surrealist Exhibition in London in 1936. Now in the Tate collection, her *Angel of Anarchy* (1936-40) is a sculpted plaster head, dressed with African beads, shells, feathers and other found ornaments, and with its eyes blindfolded with a strip of cloth. Agar and her friend Henry Moore were frequent visitors to the British Museum, and both were inspired in different ways by the collection of African Art. Agar started *Angel of Anarchy* in the first year of the Spanish Civil War, at a time when she and other British Surrealists felt great sympathy for the Spanish Anarchists; Herbert Reed published *The Necessity of Anarchism* in 1936. The blindfold was added in 1940, after the outbreak of the Second World War, signalling uncertainty.

# SEVEN & FIVE SOCIETY

A manifesto accompanying their exhibition at Walker's Galleries on New Bond Street in April 1920 explained that in place of 'a new –ism' the Seven & Five Society espoused a return to calm: 'there has of late been too much pioneering along too many lines in altogether too much of a hurry.' This changed with the arrival of Ben and Winifred Nicholson in 1924. Interest shifted to a naïve aesthetic that rejected academic influence, inspired by Ben Nicolson's 'discovery' of Alfred Wallis, a former St Ives fisherman, who's untutored style held great appeal. As Nicholson assumed presidency of the society in 1926, his sway grew; in came ideas from Europe, a shift toward abstraction and members Henry Moore, John Piper and Barbara Hepworth. In 1932, Nicholson and Hepworth embarked on an affair and travelled to France, pitching themselves excitedly into a world of pioneering new –isms. In 1934, Nicholson's attempt to change the society's name to the 7 & 5 Abstract Group led to mass exodus. Nevertheless, the following year, the group held London's first exhibition of entirely abstract works. It was also the Group's last: the 7 & 5 disbanded, splintered by modernist convictions and tangled personal relationships.

## WADDINGTON CUSTOT
**11 Cork Street, W1S 3LT**
waddingtoncustot.com

The gallery formerly known as Waddington opened on Cork Street in 1958, showing work by contemporary British artists including Patrick Heron, Elisabeth Frink and William Turnbull. Waddington partnered with French dealer Stephane Custot in 2011, and shows modern and contemporary art, with a solid foundation of British names from the latter twentieth century.

# AUCTION HOUSES

## BONHAMS
**Montpelier Street, SW7 1HH
AND
101 New Bond Street, W1S 1SR**
bonhams.com

Founded in Covent Garden by a print dealer in the 1790s, Bonhams survived the wartime bombing of two subsequent sites. It only moved to its Bond Street headquarters in 2001, and proudly declares itself the only international auction house still 'privately owned and in British hands.' Lots up for auction are on view in the week before, and there's a Michelin-starred restaurant on site serving wines purchased from its sales. A second site in Knightsbridge is known for jewellery.

## PHILLIPS
**30 Berkeley Square, W1J 6EX**
phillips.com

Founded in the 1790s, Phillips has gone through decades (centuries, even) of mergers, acquisitions and name changes. It reverted to its original – and current – moniker in 2013, and opened its pointedly modern headquarters on Berkeley Square the following year. Modern and contemporary art and design is the focus, and on show in big shopfront galleries. Despite over two centuries of history, Phillips has opted to position itself as the hip young gunslinger on the (auction) block.

## SOTHEBY'S
**34-35 New Bond Street, W1A 2AA**
sothebys.com

Founded in 1744, Sotheby's moved to Bond Street – the heart of the artworld at the time – in 1917. Hitherto specialising in rare books, in the years between the wars, Sotheby's focus shifted to fine and decorative arts. Today the auction house holds sales around the world, in categories ranging from toys to cars. Exhibitions of art up for auction are open to view in the days ahead of the major sales.

# PUBLIC ARTWORKS

**ELISABETH FRINK,**
***HORSE AND RIDER* (1974-5)**
Corner of New Bond Street and Burlington Gardens, W1S 3LU

Frink returned to equestrian subjects throughout her career. This naked figure, mounted bareback without a harness, suggests strength and harmony between man and horse. Frink is also responsible for the eagle on the Eagle Squadrons Memorial in nearby Grosvenor Square.

Elisabeth Frank, *Horse and Rider* (1974)

**ANTONY GORMLEY,**
*ROOM* (2014)
8 Balderton Street, Brown Hart Gardens,
W1K 6TF

Blocky sculpture of a crouched figure perched on the façade of the Beaumont Hotel by the artist famous for the *Angel of the North*. It's actually a functioning part of the hotel, with a cave-like suite inside that you can rent for £1,260 a night.

**IAN HAMILTON FINDLAY,**
*UNTITLED* (2003-5)
21 Davies Street, W1K 3DE

Hamilton Findlay inscribed quotations from the French revolutionary Louis Antoine de Saint-Just into the terracotta façade at 21 Davies Street.

**HENRY MOORE,**
*TIME-LIFE SCREEN* (1952-3)
153-7 New Bond Street, W1S 2TY

Moore designed the four stone sculptures on the façade as integral to the screen they stand in. 'The fact that it is only a screen with space behind it, led me to carve it with a back as well as a front, and to pierce it, which gives an interesting penetration of light,' Moore later wrote. The dynamic bronze sculpture *Symbol of Community* by Maurice Lambert is mounted above the entry doors.

# GEOMETRY OF FEAR

Spikey, precariously balanced, technologically sophisticated and riven with anxiety, the post-war mood was writ large and three dimensional in the work of the generation of British sculptors that came to prominence in the early 1950s. Lynn Chadwick, Eduardo Paolozzi, Rex Butler and Bernard Meadows were among those chosen to represent Britain at the Venice Biennale of 1952. Critic Herbert Read's review ran heavy on references to the work of T.S. Eliot: 'These new images belong to the iconography of despair, or of defiance; and the more innocent the artist, the more effectively he transmits the collective guilt. Here are images of flight, or ragged claws "scuttling across the floors of silent seas", of excoriated flesh, frustrated sex, the geometry of fear.'

# ST JAMES'S

## INSTITUTIONS

**ICA**
The Mall, SW1Y 5AH
ica.art

It is a delightful quirk of London that one of its most subversive institutions shares a street with the Queen. Fiercely contemporary, with an eye to the margins rather than the mainstream, the ICA is a site for talks, events, music and cinema as well as art, much of it at the progressive, and often controversial, cutting edge. Free entry Tuesdays. Outstanding restaurant and bookstore.

**MALL GALLERIES**
The Mall, SW1
mallgalleries.org.uk

Exhibition venue and home to the Federation of British Artist Societies, the Mall Galleries host a program of shows and competitions largely dedicated to representational art.

**THE NATIONAL GALLERY**
Trafalgar Square, WC2N 5DN
nationalgallery.org.uk

National collection of European paintings, with works dating from the thirteenth to early twentieth centuries. Star turns include Jan van Eyck's *Arnolfini Portrait* (1434), Diego Velazquez's *The Toilet of Venus* (aka the 'Rokeby Venus', 1647-51), *The Ambassadors* (1533) by Hans Holbein the Younger, and works by Leonardo, Rembrandt, Rubens and van Gogh. A recently acquired self-portrait by Artemisia Gentileschi was only the twentieth work by a female artist in a collection of 2,300 paintings. Collection free, exhibitions ticketed.

**THE NATIONAL PORTRAIT GALLERY**
St Martin's Place, WC2H 0HE
npg.org.uk

Founded as a collection of portraits of 'men and women who have made and are making British history and culture,' the collection now extends to over 200,000 portraits, including painted, photographic and even moving image. In the summer and winter months, the gallery hosts exhibitions of works shortlisted for painted and photographic portrait awards. Collection free, exhibitions ticketed.

The National Gallery, Trafalgar Square

The National Portrait Gallery, St Martin's Place

# KENNETH CLARK

Recruited to the post in 1933, Clark was, at 30, the youngest director of the National Gallery, and oversaw the institution until the end of the war in 1945. Greatly admired as a writer and academic, Clark was committed to the ideal of making art accessible to all, both by opening institutions up to all audiences, and communicating his own knowledge clearly and with passion. It was this latter skill that made Clark a star through the 1960s television series *Civilisation*. Clark's vision of great art – white, European, male – may seem superannuated, but his contribution to British culture was profound, from persuading the government to employ hundreds of artists during the war, to championing the work of Henry Moore, to his instrumental role in what would later become the Arts Council of England.

# THE INDEPENDENT GROUP

Between 1952 and 55, a group of artists, architects and writers met in the Members Room of the ICA – then on Dover Street – fascinated by the image-saturated cultural landscape emerging in the post-war years. Hollywood cinema, popular music, American cars, glamorous adverts and sci-fi comics were discussed on equal footing with modern art, design and architecture. Leading figures included artists Richard Hamilton, Eduardo Paolozzi and William Turnbull, architects Alison and Peter Smithson and critic Lawrence Alloway. Using collage, found objects and printmaking, their art reacted against the elitism of high culture. The Independent Group laid the foundations for Pop Art in Britain, and was at the core of the conceptual 1956 show *This Is Tomorrow* at the Whitechapel Art Gallery.

# MARC QUINN'S *SELF*

Arguably the most unconventional likeness held at the National Portrait Gallery is a cast of Marc Quinn's head formed from eight pints of the artist's frozen blood. Maintained at a sub-zero temperature in its own refrigeration unit, *Self* is the third in a series of self-portraits commenced in 1991, and updated at five-year intervals. Each marks the passage of time, in the artist's face, and in data stored in the blood. Quinn has continued to explore ideas of contemporary portraiture, creating series based on retina photographs, fingerprints and 3D scanning; prescient for a world that values personal data as a saleable commodity.

# THE NATIONAL GALLERY IN WARTIME

In 1938, with war looming and with it, the threat of bombardment, the question arose of how to protect masterpieces held at the National Gallery. In the ten days preceding the declaration of war on 3 September 1939, the entire collection was removed, according to plan, and transported to locations in Wales. In 1940, fearing invasion, director Kenneth Clark visited Winston Churchill and proposed it be shipped to Canada, an idea the Prime Minister rejected, suggesting instead it be hidden underground. Protective chambers were constructed in an old slate mine at Blaenau Ffestiniog at Manod, where the collection was stored from 1941 until the end of the war. The Gallery remained open, despite sustaining bomb damage, and hosted lunchtime concerts and temporary exhibitions. In 1942, as the bombing lessened, one painting a month was brought up from Manod, displayed during the day, and cached underground at night.

# MARY BEALE

Britain's first female professional portraitist was born in Suffolk in 1633, the daughter of a keen amateur painter. It is thought she met the fashionable portrait artist Peter Lely as a child. She certainly acquired technique by copying works by Lely, and watched him in his studio; he, in return, took some interest in promoting her. Aged 18, she married Charles Beale, a cloth merchant and amateur painter who, recognising his wife's superior talents, supported her in launching a career. Referring to his wife throughout as 'my dearest heart', Charles Beale filled some 30 notebooks detailing her sitters, fees and the techniques she employed. He also prepared her canvases, and greeted clients to the studio. Beale was deft in catching nuance of character, particularly in children. Perhaps her best portraits are of her husband Charles, who she shows with somewhat misty-eyed affection in 1680, his shirt falling open at the chest and his hair tumbling in natural curls. This is thought to be the companion painting to Beale's self-portrait – now in the collection of the National Portrait Gallery – in which she shows herself as both artist and mother, her right hand propped on a half-finished painting of her two sons.

# NEW ENGLISH ART CLUB

Founded in 1886 as a progressive counterbalance to the Royal Academy, the New English is an elected society of painters that counted John Singer Sargent and Walter Sickert among its founders, and subsequently many artists associated with Bloomsbury and Camden Town. In early decades, the New English was strongly influenced by recent developments in France – Impressionist and Post-Impressionist painting. The tendency to figuration endured, if not the progressive reputation: by the early twentieth century the New English was seen as a springboard for election to the Royal Academy. The Club is still active, holding an annual exhibition at the Mall Galleries.

# THE ICA

The Institute of Contemporary Art was founded in London's bleak post-war years by a group that included surrealist Roland Penrose and critic Herbert Read, who together organised the first two ICA exhibitions in the basement under a cinema on Oxford Street. The ICA expanded in 1950 into 17 Dover Street (the building would, many years later, house the Dover Street Market fashion emporium), and again in 1968, into its current site on The Mall. Since its early days, the ICA has suffered the tension implicit in the requirement that it teeter on the cultural cutting edge without falling into catastrophic debt. Risky business.

# LUBAINA HIMID AND THE THIN BLACK LINE

In the 1980s, young artist Lubaina Himid pushed back against the limited opportunities offered to Black artists by the establishment, organising important exhibitions of work by female contemporaries. Five Black Women at the Africa Centre (1983), Black Women Time Now at Battersea Arts Centre (1983-4) and The Thin Black Line at the ICA in 1984 made a powerful case for the work of Sonia Boyce, Claudette Johnson, Ingrid Pollard, Maud Sulter and Himid herself. Some three decades later, as a new generation of curators replaces elements of the conservative old guard, Himid and those she championed have started to achieve long overdue recognition. In 2017, following a change permitting nomination of artists over the age of 50, Himid won the Turner Prize, and in 2019 was elected RA.

# COMMERCIAL GALLERIES

**ALAN CRISTEA**
43 Pall Mall, SW1Y 5JG
alancristea.com

Specialising in artist prints and editions, as well as original works. Now represents the estates of a number of artists prominent in the late twentieth century, such as Richard Hamilton and Howard Hodgkin, alongside a Brit-heavy roster of major names, among them Michael Craig-Martin, Joe Tilson and Julian Opie.

**BEN HUNTER**
1 Princes Place, Duke Street, SW1Y 6DE
benhunter.gallery

Young and energetic gallery on two upper floors, down an alleyway along the back of Christie's.

**BERNARD JACOBSON GALLERY**
28 Duke Street, SW1Y 6AG
jacobsongallery.com

Jacobson started publishing and making artist prints in 1969; since then he's worked with a startling list from both sides of the Atlantic, including Helen Frankenthaler, Ed Ruscha, Kurt Schwitters, Howard Hodgkin and Bruce McLean.

**GROSVENOR GALLERY**
35 Bury Street, SW1Y 6AY
grosvenorgallery.com

Founded by American sociologist and collector Eric Estorick in 1960, Grosvenor went beyond the mainstream, showing art from Russia and Eastern Europe, as well as British artists including Francis Newton Souza and Prunella Clough. Now focused on modern art from South Asia.

**HAZLITT HOLLAND-HIBBERT**
38 Bury Street, SW1Y 6BB
hh-h.com

An all-Brits list here. HHH show big names, from Bridget Riley to David Hockney, most working in the twentieth century.

**JACK BELL**
13 Mason's Yard, SW1Y 6BU
jackbellgallery.com

International-minded gallery representing interesting younger artists from Africa and East Asia (largely figurative painters), among them Boris Nzebo, Baatarzorig Batjargal and Jean David Nkot, as well as veteran photographer Hamidou Maiga.

## SKARSTEDT
8 Bennet Street, SW1A 1RP
skarstedt.com

London outpost for New York-based dealer with an appetite for work from the 1980s New York scene, and artists who emerged in the era, among them Eric Fischl, David Salle, Jenny Holzer, Cindy Sherman and Richard Prince.

## THOMAS DANE
3 Duke Street, SW1Y 6BN
AND
11 Duke Street, SW1Y 6BN
thomasdanegallery.com

The gallerist says he opened his first space on Duke Street in 2004 when artist (now film-maker) Steve McQueen asked Dane to represent him. Dane has since opened a space in Naples, a city he feels his artists will be excited to show in. Beside McQueen, Brits in his international line-up include Anthea Hamilton, Anya Gallaccio, Michael Landy and Caragh Thuring.

## WHITE CUBE
25-26 Mason's Yard
London SW1Y 6BU
AND
144-152 Bermondsey Street, SE1 3TQ
whitecube.com

Indelibly associated with the Young British Artists who exploded onto the London scene in the early 1990s, Jay Jopling's White Cube Gallery today presents itself as a heavy hitter on the international scene. Two slick spaces in London and a third in Hong Kong support a roster from around the world, with an exhibition program that would be the envy of many museums. There's still space on Jopling's list for Damien Hirst and Tracey Emin, but few other mementoes of the early years.

# AUCTION HOUSES

## CHRISTIE'S
8 King Street, SW1Y 6QT
christies.com

James Christie opened his salesroom on Pall Mall in 1766, overseeing historic auctions of the age, including items from the collection of Sir Robert Walpole, sold to Catherine the Great of Russia. The House moved to its current King Street location in 1823, and now has ten salesrooms around the world. Works are typically installed in the showroom three or four days before an auction and all are welcome to view.

# WHITE CUBE

In 1993, Jay Jopling – hitherto a dynamo behind temporary exhibitions in locations including his own flat – brokered an agreement with Christie's to take over a room at 44 Duke Street to show work by artists of the new generation. In May of that year White Cube arrived with a bang: a full-page advertisement in *Frieze* magazine, a show by Goldsmiths' graduate Itai Doron, and queues up the stairs to get into the tiny first-floor gallery. Crowds drinking Becks thronged the street on opening nights, and continued on to the Chequers Tavern. Artists on White Cube's opening list included Damien Hirst, Gavin Turk and Marc Quinn. Over the ten years he was on Duke Street, Jopling also mounted shows by Jake & Dinos Chapman, Tracey Emin, Marcus Harvey, Gary Hume and Sam Taylor Wood, linking White Cube indelibly with the British art boom of the 1990s.

# INDICA

In 1965, London's art scene got a jolt of new life with the arrival of Indica, an alternative bookshop and gallery, at 6 Mason's Yard. Started by Barry Miles, Peter Asher and John Dunbar, the gallery took its name from *Cannabis Indica* and its clientele – artists and visitors alike – were appropriately switched on. Over the two years it was open, Indica showed Julio Le Parc, Liliane Lijn, Takis, Lourdes Castro, Jesús Rafael Soto and Carlos Cruz-Diez. Recently graduated from Cambridge University, Dunbar and his partners in Indica became cultural superconnectors within a city thrilling to its own creative energy. Paul McCartney was an early customer, and lent a hand setting up. Glamour came, too, courtesy of Dunbar's young wife, the singer Marianne Faithfull, then in her first burst of pop stardom. Indica's private views packed Mason's Yard with an exciting crowd drawn from London's counterculture. An artist himself, Dunbar hung out with the Beat Generation poets, drank cocktails at Peggy Guggenheim's Palazzo in Venice, and connected with artists from the Fluxus movement, among them Yoko Ono. It was at Ono's exhibition at Indica in 1967 that the artist first met John Lennon, handing him a card that read 'breathe'.

# THE FOURTH PLINTH

Since 1999, the empty plinth at the north-west corner of Trafalgar Square has hosted a series of contemporary sculptures, starting with Mark Wallinger's *Ecce Homo*, a life-sized figure of Christ dwarfed by the huge plinth. Each stays in place for 18 months. Installed in 2018, Michael Rakowitz presented *The Invisible Enemy Should Not Exist*, a winged bull from Niniveh that had been destroyed by ISIS in 2015, recreated using empty Iraqi date syrup cans. In 2020-21, the plinth is home to Heather Phillipson's *The End*, an outsized blob of cream holding a massive cherry, both threatening to topple off their base, and under attack from a fly and a surveillance drone.

The Fourth Plinth; Michael Rakowitz, *The Invisible Enemy Should Not Exist* (2018)

# GLUCK

As a young woman, Gluck rejected her family name along with the dress and confines of her gender. In short hair and sharp, tailored suits she cut a dash through the London art world of the 1920s and 30s. Born Hannah Gluckstein, to a wealthy Jewish family, Gluck's mannish garb and refusal to comply with the behavioural codes of her time troubled her father, but he nevertheless provided her with the financial support for an elegant, artistic life. Gluck had a custom-built studio and frequented the theatre and cabaret; performance provided a theme for Stage and Country, her first exhibition. A passionate romance with influential florist Constance Spry brought with it a mania for plant and flower portraits. It was Gluck's subsequent love affair with socialite Nesta Obermer – immortalised in the double portrait *Medallion* – that she saw as a true twinning of souls, though it caused her both joy and heartache. Critically admired and commercially successful in the 1920s and 30s, by the post-war period Gluck had fallen out of vogue. Living away from Nesta and the thrilling hubbub of London, she suffered decades of block and frustration before a final, magnificent burst of energy in the late 1960s.

# NICHOLAS HILLIARD

It was training as a goldsmith that delivered Nicholas Hilliard his meticulous hand, and his subsequent ability to work marvels on a 5cm disc of vellum – his 'pictures in little' – that brought him to the Royal Court. Born in Exeter in 1547, Hilliard became miniaturist to Queen Elizabeth I, James I and their courts. Portraits 'in little' were commissioned as intimate gifts: courtship, romantic and diplomatic. Their portability allowed the image of the sitter to travel. Hilliard held Albrecht Dürer and Hans Holbein as artist heroes, writing: 'Holbein's manner of limning I have ever imitated, and hold it for the best.' He worked on vellum burnished back and front with a dog's tooth, mounted on a stiff playing card. Pigment bound with gum arabic was applied with a squirrel-hair brush known as a 'Pensill.' Hilliard occupied a pivotal position in re-defining portraiture as a 'gentle' (ie, gentlemanly) pursuit. In an era when artists were seen as journeymen, and few paintings were signed, he stands as the first great British-born portraitist, and author of the first great English art treaties, the *Arte of Limning* (c.1600). (The word 'limning' derived from illumination, and was used to describe fine miniature work.)

# WESTMINSTER

## INSTITUTIONS

### PALACE OF WESTMINSTER
SW1A 0AA
parliament.uk

There has been a curator here since the Palace was rebuilt after a fire in 1834, and the collection of 8,500 works includes medieval statuary, ministerial portraits and works of political satire. Some you can visit, some you can't, though all are listed in an online archive. Inevitably, the investigation of what art is collected, how, and why, leads straight down a rabbit hole of advisory committees, cross-party groups and acquisition policies.

### PARLIAMENT SQUARE
SW1P 3BD

The public square-cum-traffic island opposite the Palace of Westminster is home to statues of politically notable figures, among them Prime Ministers Benjamin Disraeli and Winston Churchill, and Nelson Mandela, Mahatma Gandhi and Millicent Fawcett.

### QUEEN'S GALLERY
Buckingham Palace, SW1A 1AA
rct.uk

Purpose-built gallery to the side of Buckingham Palace showing changing exhibitions of works from the vast Royal Collection, largely accumulated since the restoration of the monarchy in 1660. Works range from drawings by Leonardo and Michelangelo, through Dutch and Flemish paintings, royal portraits and early British photography, to decorative arts and antiques. Ticketed.

### SAINT MARGARET'S CHURCH
St Margaret Street, SW1P 3JX
westminster-abbey.org

In 1967, John Piper's stained glass window designs – silvery-grey panels broken up with shards of greens and yellow – were installed in eight bays of the south aisle, replacing windows broken during the Second World War.

## WESTMINSTER ABBEY
20 Deans Yd, SW1P 3PA
westminster-abbey.org

For centuries the site of royal coronations and interments, the Gothic abbey at Westminster dates back to 1245, and occupies land that housed Benedictine monks in the tenth century. There are wall paintings and carvings that date back to its earliest decades, and a number of significant portraits, including Richard II from c.1395. Artists honoured in the Abbey have snuck in, through verse, to Poet's Corner, among them William Blake and Edward Lear.

# EUROPEAN PAINTERS
# TO THE ROYAL COURT

The King or Queen's Painter was the conduit through which a monarch and their court were seen; portraits circulated as diplomatic gifts and precursors to courtship, and were displayed to broadcast majesty in its full expression. The painters responsible for the public image of British monarchs in the sixteenth and seventeenth centuries were overwhelmingly Flemish. Many were refugees from religious persecution. Meynnart Wewyck painted the court of Henry VII, Lucas Horenbout was King's painter and miniaturist to Henry VIII, superseded by the great German-born painter Hans Holbein the Younger. He had left Europe for London on the recommendation of the Dutch philosopher Erasmus, who put him in contact with Lord Chancellor Sir Thomas More, explaining: 'The arts are freezing in this part of the world and he is on the way to England to pick up some angels.' Elizabeth I was an exception: her stiff, coruscating grandeur and the intricate symbolism of her dress were captured by the British portraitist Nicholas Hilliard, and his pupil Isaac Oliver. The following century brought Daniel Mytens, Peter Lely (born Pieter van der Faes in Westphalia) and the mighty Anthony van Dyck, the dandyish, lavish sensuality of whose portraiture incarnates the image of Charles I's court.

# PUBLIC ART

## 55 BROADWAY
SW1H 0BD

London's first building constructed in the steel-framed 'sky-scraper' style, Charles Holden's 1929 art deco block sits above St James's Park underground station, the headquarters of the Underground Electric Railways Company. Reliefs and sculptures commissioned for the Portland Stone façade include evocations of the four winds by Eric Gill, Eric Aumonier, Samuel Rabinovitch and Henry Moore, and primitivist figures of *Day* and *Night* by Jacob Epstein. Epstein's figures – graphic, naked and lowering – caused such scandal that a campaign was launched for their removal. The sculptures remain, though 4cm was carved off the penis of the young boy in *Day*.

## AUGUSTE RODIN, *THE BURGHERS OF CALAIS* (1889)
Victoria Tower Gardens, Millbank, SW1P 3JA

One of four casts of Rodin's sculpture commissioned by the city of Calais, this was purchased by the National Art Fund in 1911, and its installation overseen by the artist himself; Rodin was a frequent visitor to London, and devotee of its museums. Commemorating the 1347 siege of Calais during the Hundred Years War between England and France, the sculpture shows the six councilmen, led by Eustache de Saint-Pierre, who offered up their lives in return for those of their fellow citizens.

# BRIAN HAW'S PEACE CAMP

On 2 June 2001, Brian Haw set up a one-man peace camp in Parliament Square in response to British government sanctions against Iraq. Legal action of many kinds was taken against Haw, his growing display of placards and protest objects, and use of a loudhailer. He spent long periods in court defending his right to protest. In May 2006, 78 police officers removed all but one of Haw's placards. Artist Mark Wallinger meticulously recreated Haw's protest site for the central Duveen Gallery of Tate Britain, which opened in January 2007 under the title *State Britain*. Haw remained in position until 2010, despite arrest, injury and lengthy wrangles with the Serious Organised Crime and Police Act.

Auguste Rodin's *The Burghers of Calais* (1889)

# GILLIAN WEARING
## and Millicent Fawcett

Wearing's early work in the 1990s engaged with the public realm. In *Signs that say what you want them to say and not Signs that say what someone else wants you to say* (1992-3) Londoners were photographed holding self-penned placards, among them 'I'm Desperate' and 'I have been certified as mildly insane.' For *Dancing in Peckham* (1994), Wearing filmed herself in a shopping mall, dancing uninhibitedly in silence for 25 minutes. *Confess All On Video. Don't Worry, You Will Be In Disguise. Intrigued? Call Gillian...* (1994) started with an ad in *Time Out* magazine; those who responded were filmed in wigs and masks, a modern take on the Catholic confessional. More recent work has explored the composite nature of identity, with the artist photographing herself masked and disguised as family members and figures she admires, among them Georgia O'Keeffe, Marcel Duchamp and Diane Arbus. Wearing's statue commemorating suffragist Millicent Fawcett was unveiled in 2018, on the centenary of the 1918 Representation of the People Act. The first statue of a woman in Parliament Square, Fawcett is presented much like a figure from Wearing's earlier portrait series, holding aloft a sign reading 'Courage Calls To Courage Everywhere.'

# MARYLEBONE

## INSTITUTIONS

**AMBIKA P3**
35 Marylebone Road, NW1 5LS
p3exhibitions.com

Dramatic subterranean space once used as a concrete construction hall by the engineering department of the University of Westminster, now an event and exhibition venue. Regular fixtures include the Sunday art fair in October, and the arty experimental London Contemporary Music Festival in December.

**THE WALLACE COLLECTION**
Hertford House, Manchester Square
W1U 3BN
wallacecollection.org

Gorgeous works by Rembrandt, Velázquez, Rubens, Fragonard, Frans Hals, and Canaletto hang in an interior dressed with exquisitely crafted furniture, Sèvres porcelain and armour. Temporary exhibitions explore modern works with an affinity to the collection. Collection free, exhibitions ticketed.

## SIR RICHARD AND LADY WALLACE

The Wallace Collection was left to the nation by Lady Wallace in 1897, according to the wishes of her late husband. Born Richard Jackson, Sir Wallace was likely the illegitimate son of the 4th Marquess of Hertford, a prodigious collector living in Paris, for whom the younger man worked as private secretary, managing – and eventually inheriting – his collection and properties. On the death of the Marquess in 1871 Richard Wallace was finally able to marry Julie-Amélie-Charlotte Castelnau, the one-time *parfumerie* assistant who had been his mistress for over 30 years. So large was the collection in Hertford House that the couple temporarily placed a portion of it on display at the Bethnal Green Museum where it received over two million visitors. Moved back to the newly extended Hertford House in 1875, the collection remained accessible; signatures in the visitors' book include Benjamin Disraeli, Auguste Rodin, Isabella Stewart Gardner, Thomas Hardy and Elizabeth Garrett Anderson.

# COMMERCIAL GALLERIES

**THE GALLERY OF EVERYTHING**
4 Chiltern Street, W1U 7PS
gallevery.com

The selling arm of the nomadic Museum of Everything, dedicated to what used dismissively to be called 'Outsider Art': work by artists who have received no formal training, and who operate outside the mainstream artworld. The results are consistently interesting, often inspiring.

# PUBLIC ART

**BARBARA HEPWORTH,**
*WINGED FIGURE* (1963)
Holles Street, W1C 1DX

A massive work by the eminent twentieth-century sculptor, evoking the dynamism of flight – bird or angel – as well as the protective shelter of a pair of arching wings.

**EDWARD BURNE-JONES,**
**WINDOWS OF ST PETER'S**
**(C. 1883)**
Vere Street, W1G 0DQ

Built between 1721-24 according to designs by James Gibbs (a precursor to the architect's grander project for St Martin's in the Fields in 1726), the renovation of St Peter's in the Victorian period included the commission of stained-glass windows, designed by Edward Burne-Jones and created by Morris & Co.

# EMILY MARY OSBORN AND *NAMELESS AND FRIENDLESS*

Presented at the Royal Academy in 1857, *Nameless and Friendless* depicts an anxious and bedraggled young orphan showing a painting to a sceptical London dealer. Osborn makes her position as a lone woman in London evident: behind her two men apparently examining a print of a ballerina are eyeing her with questionable intent. 'The theme […] is innocence, delicious feminine innocence, exposed to the world,' wrote Linda Nochlin. 'It is the charming vulnerability of the young woman artist, like that of the hesitating model, which is really the subject of Osborn's painting, not the value of the young woman's work or her pride in it: the issue here is, as usual, sexual rather than serious.' The position of women in the artworld and society were abiding themes for Osborn. She was of a generation for whom the Royal Academy Schools and study of the nude were unavailable, severely limiting her prospects. Osborn was a close associate of activist Barbara Bodichon and a member of the Langham Place Circle that fought for women's rights, education and suffrage; in 1859 the group petitioned the Royal Academy for access to the Schools. Osborn lived in St John's Wood with her companion Mary Elizabeth Dunn.

# ART ON THE UNDERGROUND

Covering every commission by Art on The Underground since it was set up in 2000 would take another book in itself. Over the years, they have proved themselves a bold commissioning body, installing Heather Phillipson's wild video-game-like sculpture *my name is lettie eggsyrub* along the whole of a disused platform at Gloucester Road Station in 2018, a suggestive cladding by collage artist Linder around Southwark station, and a network-wide project by Laure Prouvost the following year. Some of the commissions are permanent, becoming part of the stations' architecture; others, such as Njideka Akunyili Crosby's magnificent mural for Brixton Station, are alas only in situ for a limited period. For the 150th anniversary of the network in 2013, Mark Wallinger created a circular labyrinth (a play on the network's roundel logo, as well as the network's map) to be installed in each of the 270 underground stations. Every six months, an artist is commissioned to create a cover for the paper tube map: they also hand out art maps. Used by 1.35 billion passengers a year, the tube network is, if you will excuse the pun, an extraordinary platform for contemporary art.

# J.M.W. TURNER

Born the son of a Covent Garden barber in 1775, Joseph Mallord William Turner's restless desire to observe, experience and translate elemental forces into paint raised him to the height of acclaim in his lifetime. It also pushed him beyond it, into realms of experimentation that few contemporaries would follow. That is to say: Turner was excited by water and sky, and fluctuations of light passing through them. An engraver he worked with on the many popular print editions of his drawings remembered Turner spending hours on Hampstead Heath 'studying the effects of atmosphere and the changes of light and shade, and the gradations required to express them.' His desire to capture this ceaseless movement in paint drove him progressively further and further from the idealised, classically inspired landscape tradition.

In his early teens, Turner enrolled in the Royal Academy Schools at Somerset House, working at the same time producing drawings for an architect's office and as a scenic artist for theatre. During holiday periods he travelled around Britain, sketching land and seascapes that he annotated as the basis for future drawings and paintings, produced to order. He travelled tirelessly to the end of his life, both around Britain and across Western Europe, through the Low Countries, then across the Alps to Venice.

In 1799, Turner was elected an Associate of the Royal Academy and moved to Harley Street. Here he lived and worked, assisted by his devoted father. In 1804, Turner opened a gallery on the first floor to show work to select clients. While he referred to it dismissively as the 'shop,' and relied on it for much of his income, Turner disliked selling paintings and thought of his canvasses as family. Later, he bought back much of his earlier work at auction, and stipulated in his will that his paintings be kept together as a gift to the nation.

Turner progressively expanded the gallery, giving it a separate entrance on Queen Anne Street. He lived for periods on the Thames, at Hammersmith and Twickenham, and converted two houses in Wapping into The Ship and Bladebone public house. In 1846, he moved into a home at Cremorne Road in Chelsea with the widow Sophia Caroline Booth. They lived happily, as if man and wife – Turner was known locally as Admiral Booth – and it was here he died in 1851. He left his paintings to the National Gallery on the proviso that they erected rooms to house them in his name – otherwise the paintings would remain at Queen Anne Street. They are now housed at Tate Britain.

# MICHAEL LANDY'S
## *Break Down*

In 2001, Michael Landy installed a material reclamation facility within Oxford Street's defunct C&A department store. Over two weeks, all the artist's possessions were fed along its conveyor belt and efficiently destroyed by a team in blue overalls. Ranging from love letters and photographs to a SAAB car, it had taken Landy a year to catalogue each of the 7,227 items that would subsequently be fed through *Break Down*. All passed beneath the gaze of the spectating public, neatly catalogued in clear numbered envelopes. On the London street dedicated to ceaseless consumption, Landy was eventually left as a man with no possessions. Structures of consumption and destruction are an abiding theme in his work. In *Market* (1990) he presented empty stalls from a London fruit n' veg market as a suite of sculptures. *Scrapheap Services* (1995) was a fictional cleaning organisation – motto 'We leave the scum with no place to hide' – which collected and disposed of little human figures Landy had spent two years cutting out of waste packaging. More recently the artist has taken aim at the consumer cycle of the art world itself, installing his *Art Bin* for the disposal of unwanted works at the South London Gallery in 2010.

# FITZROVIA

## INSTITUTIONS

### FITZROVIA CHAPEL
**Fitzroy Place, 2 Pearson Square**
**W1T 3BF**
fitzroviachapel.org

Formerly part of the (now demolished) Middlesex Hospital, this unconsecrated Gothic revival chapel is lavishly decorated in marble and gold mosaic. Restored and re-opened (amid a ton of local development) in 2015, it now hosts exhibitions and art events as well as secular weddings.

### RIBA
**66 Portland Place, W1B 1AD**
architecture.com

The temple-like art deco building housing the Royal Institute of British Architects was designed by George Grey Wornum and opened in 1934, a century after the organisation received its royal charter. A free public gallery shows architectural and arty crossover exhibitions and there is a strong talks program.

## COMMERCIAL GALLERIES

### ALISON JACQUES
**16-18 Berners Street, W1T 3LN**
alisonjacquesgallery.com

A favourite with London's feminist critics. Alison Jacques's small but mighty gallery shows a punchy mix of out-there photography – Juergen Teller, Robert Mapplethorpe – and contemporary painting. The star attractions, though, are artists of the feminist avant-garde including Hannah Wilke and Ana Mendieta, and blossoming late-career artists such as Sheila Hicks.

### EDEL ASSANTI
**74a Newman Street, W1T 3DB**
edelassanti.com

First launched as an itinerant project space, this is a young gallery with a roster of punky, outspoken artists from around the world, making politically and socially engaged work.

# THE MACLAREN-ROSS CIRCUIT

In the early, war-wrecked decades of the twentieth century, it was to Fitzrovia that London's bohemia came to drink, plot, argue, talk and flirt, but mainly drink. The area took its name from the Fitzroy Tavern, where artists, poets, composers, writers and their circle downed brandy alongside an eccentric cast of local characters. Augustus John, Wyndham Lewis, and Nina Hamnett (the 'Queen of Bohemia') arrived in Fitzrovia after studying at the nearby Slade School. Among other notables were poet Dylan Thomas, artists' model Betty May, notorious occultist Aleister Crowley and the novelists Anthony Powell and Malcolm Lowry. Fitzrovia seeped into their art and their writing. Powell based the glamorous but dissolute novelist X. Trapnel in *A Dance to the Music of Time* on the writer Julian Maclaren-Ross, a self-mythologising dandy drunk. After the Fitzroy Tavern became aggravatingly popular, Powell also nicknamed the pubs they favoured in his honour: the Maclaren-Ross Circuit took in The Black Horse, Bricklayers Arms, Wheatsheaf and Marquis of Granby. A deft but unfocussed writer, Maclaren-Ross died aged 52 after receiving an unexpected royalty cheque that he invested, fatally, in a bottle of brandy, consumed in one sitting.

# THE OMEGA WORKSHOPS

Alarmed by the poverty in which his artist friends were living, in 1913 artist and critic Roger Fry established a workshop at 33 Fitzroy Square in which the care and skill demanded for the creation of art might be applied to the design and production of everyday objects. Inspired by the Wiener Werkstätte, Fry's Omega Workshops Ltd. was likewise guided by the maxim that it was 'Better To Work Ten Days On One Product Than To Manufacture Ten Products In One Day.' Among the artists employed by Omega over the years were Wyndham Lewis, Edward Wadsworth, Nina Hamnett, Paul Nash, Mark Gertler, David Bomberg and Henri Gaudier-Brzeska, as well as Fry's Bloomsbury intimates Vanessa Bell and Duncan Grant. Fry shut the workshop in 1919, exhausted by the emotional firestorm that an enterprise peopled by this cast of impractical and wilful bohemians brought. The Omega aesthetic lived on in domestic spaces associated with the Bloomsbury Group, most famously in the painted interior of Charleston House, Vanessa Bell and Duncan Grant's home in Sussex.

# HENRY FUSELI

Fuseli's haunting – and enduringly popular – painting *The Nightmare* caused a sensation at the Royal Academy summer exhibition in 1782. It showed a woman 'lifeless and inanimate, thrown across the bed, her head hanging down, and her pale and distorted features half covered by hair' with a monstrous incubus squatting on her chest. Etchings and later variations by Fuseli circulated widely; the image was so well known that the dramatic scenario became a commonplace in Gothic fiction (the 'description' above is in fact no such thing; it's a scene from Mary Shelley's *Frankenstein*, published in 1818). Born Henry Füssli in Zürich, Switzerland, Fuseli studied first as a minister and was ordained in 1761. He abandoned the priesthood and travelled to London in 1764, before moving to Rome in 1770 where he trained and worked as an artist. Here he Italicised his name to Fuseli, returning to London in 1779 where he became known for his dramatic renderings of literary and mythological themes, favouring in particular scenes from Shakespeare and Milton. Fuseli was elected a Royal Academician in 1790, and served first as Professor of Painting and subsequently Keeper of the Academy Schools until his death in 1825.

# AUGUSTUS JOHN

Augustus John moved into rooms on Fitzroy Street with his sister, artist Gwen John, in 1897, after their studies at the Slade School. As a student he was already considered – by those who enjoy such hyperbolic pronouncements – the finest draftsman of his generation. The established line is that Augustus was a magnificent talent – genius, even – who failed to live up to his promise, though by all accounts, he didn't do too shabbily. Associated for a time with the Post-Impressionist Camden Town group led by Walter Sickert, John went on to become the leading portraitist of the 1920s. His reputation preceded him in other ways. Fascination with Romani culture inspired flamboyant personal style, favouring flowing hair and beard, earrings, silk scarves and a broad-brimmed hat. His personal life was equally flamboyant: to his marriage to artist Ida Nettleship in 1901, he added a common-law wife Dorelia McNeill in 1904, with whom he lived in a ménage à trois until Nettleship's death in 1907. Numerous affairs resulted in some of John's most striking and passionate portraits, notably the wild Italian heiress *Marchesa Casati* (1919) and *Lady Ottoline Morrell* (also 1919; cue fireworks). McNeill remained with John until his death in 1961.

# WYNDHAM LEWIS AND VORTICISM

By his own description a 'novelist, painter, sculptor, philosopher, draughtsman, critic, politician, journalist, essayist' and 'pamphleteer', Wyndham Lewis also displayed a talent for argument, leading to a career in which as many enterprises were commenced as were discarded prematurely. Vorticism, and its publication *Blast*, were launched from a studio in Fitzroy Street in 1914 with the assistance of poet Ezra Pound. A British response to Futurism and Cubism, it embracing the heat and speed of the machine age, and the promise of an increasingly mechanical future. The Vorticist Manifesto appeared in the first edition of *Blast*; even more influential were the magazine's bold, angular graphics. Artists associated with the movement include Henri Gaudier-Brzeska, Jacob Epstein, Dorothy Shakespear and Edward Wadsworth, and both T.S. Eliot and Ford Madox Ford contributed written material to *Blast*. With the mechanical horrors of the First World War all too present, Vorticism did not survive beyond its first exhibition in 1915; *Blast* ran for only two issues. Lewis attempted to rekindle the fire of Vorticism as Group X, formed in 1920 with William Roberts, Cuthbert Hamilton and Edward McKnight Kauffer. The group held a single exhibition in 1922, but their angular paintings of modern city scenes were out of phase – across Europe artists were turning away from avant-garde extremes in a 'return to order' (or in Germany *Neue Sachlichkeit* – new objectivity).

# THE NEO NATURISTS

'When I came up to London there were amazing-looking people with pale faces and loads of makeup,' recalls Jennifer Binnie. 'Everything was dyed hair and amazing costumes, but it didn't suit us - we couldn't do it. We wanted to be extreme, so being naked was a reaction.' Between 1981 and 1986, Binnie, her sister Christine, and Wilma Johnson performed as the Neo Naturists. At their most prolific, they appeared almost weekly at night clubs, parties and art events, collaborating with a creative circle that emerged from the squatting scene of the time, including pop stars Boy George and Marilyn, fashion designers BodyMap, dancer Michael Clark, film-makers Derek Jarman and John Maybury, artists Peter Doig, Cerith Wyn Evans and Jennifer Binnie's then-boyfriend Grayson Perry. Appearing naked but for body paint, and taped on 'bikinis' made, perhaps, from cooked prawns and crabs, Neo-Naturist performances included 'a bit of poetry reading, a bit of cooking, a bit of singing, some kind of physical jerks, yoga or a bit of housework such as sweeping up autumn leaves, apple bobbing,' recalls Johnson. 'We didn't do that much singing because I can't sing.'

## FOLD
158 New Cavendish St, W1W 6YW
foldgallery.com

New painting and sculpture by British and international artists, including Dominic Beattie, Olivia Bax, Asmund Havsteen-Mikkelsen and Valérie Kolakis, as well as invitees.

## JOSH LILLEY
44-46 Riding House Street, W1W 7EX
joshlilleygallery.com

There are some strong sculptors here – among them, Kathleen Ryan – but this is a gallery in which contemporary painting is approached with vigour, from the narrative mystery of Gareth Cadwallader's crisp tableaux to Analia Saban's 'paintings' made with concrete, vacuum-packed sachets of paint or laser cutters.

## LAURE GENILLARD
2 Hanway Place, W1T 1HB
lglondon.org

Long-established gallery showing cross-generational group shows and solos across two floors. Independent curators and live events keep fresh ideas flowing.

## NARRATIVE PROJECTS
110 New Cavendish Street, W1W 6XR
narrativeprojects.com

Daria Kirsanova's Narrative Projects put down roots in Fitzrovia in 2015 after a few nomadic years. The tendency is to larger conceptual projects, from artists including Taus Makhacheva and Patrick Hough (both already favourites on the international biennale circuit).

## PI ARTWORKS
55 Eastcastle Street, W1W 8EG
piartworks.com

London outpost of Istanbul-based gallery, with a strong list of artists Turkish and not-so-Turkish, among them Ipek Duben, Susan Hefuna and artist duo Noor Afshan Mirza and Brad Butler.

## PILAR CORRIAS
54 Eastcastle Street, W1W 8EF
pilarcorrias.com

Pilar Corrias shows big international names, among them audience-engaged relational figureheads Philippe Parreno and Rirkrit Tiravanija. It's a London home, too, to conceptual, political banner paintings by Helen Johnson, Charles Avery's documentation of his self-contained fantasy world and Ian Cheng's experiments with AI.

## REBECCA HOSSACK
28 Charlotte Street, W1T 2NA
AND
2a Conway Street, Fitzroy Square,
W1T 6BA
rebeccahossack.com

Rebecca Hossack has weathered the storm for three decades, in part because the gallery has determinedly followed its own route, among other things introducing the work of Aboriginal Australian artists to the British market.

## TIWANI CONTEMPORARY
16 Little Portland Street, W1W 8BP
tiwani.co.uk

In less than a decade Tiwani has carved a niche as the go-to gallery for exciting contemporary art from Africa and its diaspora. Their exhibitions span the generations, from new media artist Zina Saro Wiwa to photographic work exploring homoerotic desire in the context of Yoruba culture by the late Rotimi Fani-Kayode.

## TJ BOULTING
59 Riding House Street, W1W 7EG
tjboulting.com

Taking its name from the old gas and stove manufacturers that once occupied the site, TJ Boulting was opened by eclectic arts publisher Trolley Books. There's a hip list of represented artists – among them Maisie Cousins, Boo Saville and Juno Calypso – but space also for thematic curated shows.

# PUBLIC ART

## BROADCASTING HOUSE
Portland Place, W1A 1AA

The BBC's headquarters are decorated with stone sculptures and reliefs by Eric Gill; all show Ariel – he of Shakespeare's play *The Tempest* – disporting himself in various ways. The BBC committed hard to the ouchsome Ariel/Aerial pun: the tricksy spirit also lent his name to the corporation's in-house magazine.

# SOHO

## INSTITUTIONS

### THE PHOTOGRAPHER'S GALLERY
16-18 Ramillies Street, W1F 7LW
thephotographersgallery.org.uk

The home of photography in the UK is tucked away on an obscure side alley off Oxford Street. The Photographer's Gallery hosts temporary exhibitions, workshops, talks, and events. Entry to selling exhibitions of prints is free, all other exhibitions free before noon, otherwise ticketed. Excellent shop.

## COMMERCIAL GALLERIES

### AMANDA WILKINSON
First Floor, 18 Brewer Street (entrance on Green's Court), W1F 0SH
amandawilkinsongallery.com

On the first floor above the famous Lina Stores, Amanda Wilkinson shows an exciting mixed bag of works oldish and new, from art by the late filmmaker Derek Jarman to evocative paintings by Phoebe Unwin. It's an eclectic mix, but standards in this tiny space are high.

### ARCADIA MISSA
14-16 Brewer Street, First Floor
W1F 0SG
arcadiamissa.com

Through an iron gate, up a rickety staircase, through an uninviting vestibule: tiny Arcadia Missa is not much to look at, but this gallery punches WAY above its weight, working with some of the most consistently challenging and exciting young artists of the moment, including Hannah Quinlan & Rosie Hastings, Amalia Ulman, Hannah Black and Emma Talbot.

### FRITH STREET GALLERY
17-18 Golden Square, W1F 9JJ
frithstreetgallery.com
AND
Soho Square, 60 Frith Street, W1D 3JJ

It shouldn't be notable that more than half the artists represented by a major gallery are female; alas it still is. Among the stars in Frith Street's firmament: Tacita Dean, Cornelia Parker, Dayanita Singh and Marlene Dumas. There are two locations, the larger on Golden Square.

## MARIAN GOODMAN
5-8 Lower John Street, W1F 9DY
mariangoodman.com

Marian Goodman opened her first gallery in New York in 1977, introducing US audiences to European artists who have since become legendary (hello, Gerhard Richter?). She's since opened gorgeous spaces in Paris, and more recently London, where she shows thoughtful themed shows between solo displays by big names, among them Lawrence Weiner, John Baldessari, Nan Goldin and Pierre Huyghe.

# LEIGH BOWERY

'I've seen many a freak make a scene and go, but Leigh was a special kind of exhibitionist because he was dedicated and saw it as an artform,' said pop singer Boy George of Leigh Bowery. Born in Sunshine, Australia in 1961, Bowery moved to London in 1980. Nominally a fashion designer, his anarchic sensibilities placed him at the intersection of London's art, club and fashion worlds, using his body as raw material for a life that amounted to a non-stop performance. In 1985, he co-founded the club night Taboo off Leicester Square; queues would form on Thursday nights, readied for the fierce door policy: 'Dress as though your life depends on it, or don't bother.' As it progressed into ever more distorted, ever more fetishistic, ever more painted looks, Bowery's particular form of drag increasingly resembled performance art, and his audience grew. After appearing on stage with (and designing costumes for) Michael Clark's dance company, Bowery staged a week-long exhibition at the Anthony d'Offay Gallery in 1988. Each day he appeared in a new, high-concept costume – padded, masked, painted, distorted, covered head to toe in polka dots or fake fur, all attitude and poise – watched by visitors through a one-way mirror. His performances on the club circuit were not for the faint hearted. In Amsterdam he concluded a show with an on-stage enema, squirted over the audience. Another routine concluded with the 'birth' of his wife Nicola Bateman, who sloshed onto the stage accompanied by fake blood and a string of sausages. Following Bowery's performances at the d'Offay Gallery, the painter Lucian Freud suggested he might sit for a painting, which he did, regularly from 1990 up until his death at the end of 1994.

# FRANCIS BACON

Bacon did not live in Soho in the traditional sense. By preference he worked from South Kensington; from 1943, in a studio once used by the Pre-Raphaelite Sir John Everett Millais; later, in a cottage on Reece Mews, where he worked in a state of legendary chaos from 1961 until his death in 1992. But it is in Soho that he spent the time not used for painting or sleeping. 'If the spirit of a place can stimulate an artist, as I am sure it can, Soho did so for Francis,' his friend and biographer Daniel Farson wrote. Here, Bacon pursued a daily circuit taking in champagne at the 'French pub', the Colony Room and the Caves de France on Dean Street, oysters at Wheeler's on Old Compton Street, finishing off the nights at The Gargoyle Club on the corner of Meard and Dean Streets (a building now occupied by the Dean Street Townhouse.)

Born to English parents in Dublin in 1909, Bacon largely escaped formal education, and left home in 1926, travelling to Berlin and Paris before settling in London. With the guidance of artist Roy De Maistre, and a circle that included Graham Sutherland, Bacon turned fully to painting in 1933. During these early years in London, Bacon was accompanied by Jessie Lightfoot, his childhood nanny. In hard times, she would shoplift for them, and acted as a hat-check girl and lavatory attendant when Bacon held illegal gambling parties. Bacon's ghostly, skeletal *Crucifixion* of 1933 was shown that year at the Mayor gallery, and caught the attention of art critic Herbert Read (today the work is owned by Damien Hirst).

On receiving his call-up papers after the outbreak of war, Bacon hired an Alsatian dog from Harrods to exacerbate his asthma, reporting for his medical in such a state that he was granted exemption from military service.

In April 1945, he showed the work that established his reputation: *Three Studies for Figures at the Base of a Crucifixion*. Already his work was haunting, visceral, uncanny, all blind screaming mouths, smeared bruised flesh and claustrophobia. Less than a decade later, in 1954, his work was shown with Lucian Freud and Ben Nicholson in the British Pavilion at the Venice Biennale. He was honoured with two retrospectives at the Tate Gallery during his lifetime, first in 1962, then 1985.

# THE FRENCH HOUSE

The pub formerly known as York Minster acquired its nickname in the post-war years from its lavishly moustachioed proprietor Gaston Berlemont (the son of a Belgian, he was born in London the year his father took over the pub in 1914). Back in the day, the 'French pub' was a bohemian stronghold, frequented by writers and artists – among them Dylan Thomas, Brendan Behan, Lucian Freud, Francis Bacon, the photographer John Deakin, and artists' model Henrietta Moraes – alongside a heady mix of Soho regulars. The name was officially changed in 1984, after a fire at York Minster; legend has it donations for the reconstruction fund were erroneously sent to Soho. When Gaston forwarded the money, the cathedral admitted that they had, over the years, accepted wine destined for the pub. Gaston retired in 1989, but the interior is little changed, and the French continues to serve beer only by the half pint, and to attract a clientele that aspires to the bohemian reputation of its post-war heyday.

# THE COLONY ROOM

Until the late 1980s, British pubs were licenced to sell alcohol at luncheon and dinner times, closing in between. Among the Soho clubs catering to dedicated afternoon drinkers, Muriel Belcher's Colony Room was the most storied. Opened in 1949, it was a few rooms up a shabby staircase on Dean Street. Belcher – camp, foul mouthed and equipped with acid tongue – swiftly determined who was 'in' and 'out.' No matter your gender, here, the preferred pronoun was 'she', and the moniker 'cunty' deployed with affection. A loose grouping of figurative painters who drank at the Colony Room in the mid century were later bunched together by R.B. Kitaj as the London School, among them Francis Bacon, Lucian Freud, Frank Auerbach and Michael Andrews. Bacon painted several portraits of Belcher, but it is Andrews who immortalised the Colony Room itself. His painting of 1962 shows Belcher at the bar alongside Freud, Bacon, Bruce Bernard, Virginia Law and John Deakin. In the 1990s, the Colony Room became a favoured hangout of the YBAs, doing little to diminish the foul-mouthed, heavy drinking, nicotine-stained and irreverent reputation of either party. Daytime opening did for it, and the Colony Room shut in 2008, the same year the club and its alcoholic clientele were immortalised in Will Self's book *Liver*.

# MARK WALLINGER

There's plenty of London in Wallinger, and plenty of Wallinger in London; the city plays a starring role in his work. *Threshold to the Kingdom* (2000) was filmed surreptitiously at the arrivals gate of City Airport, the slow-motion emergence of airline passengers soundtracked by the sombre tones of Allegri's *Miserere. Angel* (1997) stars Islington underground station; Wallinger appears in dark glasses as his alter ego Blind Faith, walking on the bottom step of an escalator while he recites the opening of St. John's Gospel. He was the first artist to make a work for the Fourth Plinth in Trafalgar Square – *Ecce Homo* (1999) is a life-sized Christ. Hands bound, wearing a crown of barbed wire, the figure was subsequently installed on the steps of St Paul's Cathedral during the Easter period. Wallinger's work has long been critical of British nostalgia for the idealised past. His early series of racehorse portraits, *Race Class Sex* (1993), suggest the whiff of eugenics underlying the selective breeding of elite animals and the British class system. For the 150th anniversary of the London Underground, Wallinger created 270 circular labyrinths, installed as enamelled plaques at stations across the network.

## RODEO

125 Charing Cross Road, WC2H 0EW
rodeo-gallery.com

This spirited gallery first opened in Istanbul and Piraeus; now it brings a fresh perspective to London. Lodged above the Charing Cross Road, the directors welcome full-on interventions in the gallery space (a memorable show by Adriano Amaral featured bricks of stinking compost slowly dissolving into white carpeting). Buzzy Turkish and Greek artists share a roster with a thoroughly international line up.

## SADIE COLES HQ

62 Kingly Street, W1B 5QN
AND
1 Davies Street, W1K 3DB
sadiecoles.com

One of the most important homegrown London galleries, Sadie Coles launched alongside the booming London art scene of the 1990s, and still represents important figures that emerged in the era – notably Sarah Lucas. Today the gallery's outlook is global, with one of the most interesting and experimental programs in town.

## SOFT OPENING

Piccadilly Circus underground station
AND
4 Herald Street, E2 6JS
softopening.london

Within the ring-shaped concourse of Piccadilly Circus underground station; a shopfront hosting projects by emerging artists, curated by Soft Opening in Bethnal Green.

## SOUTHARD REID

7 Royalty Mews, W1D 3AS
southardreid.com

Tucked away in the corner of a less-inviting urine-scented yard, this little gallery represents some wonderful young artists. Among the favourites: photographer of uncanny situations Joanna Piotrowska, painter of the modern erotic Celia Hempton, and sideways chronicler of London's queer nightlife, Prem Sahib.

# PUBLIC ART

## JEAN COCTEAU, MURALS (1960) LADY CHAPEL, NOTRE DAME DE FRANCE

5 Leicester Place, WC2H 7BX

Cocteau's murals in this small side chapel show three episodes from the life of Mary. He was associated with the Ordre de la Rose-Croix Catholic et Esthétique du Temple et du Graal – hence the large rose placed on the cross beneath Christ's feet. Cocteau appears to the left of the cross with a falcon seated beside him.

# JEAN COCTEAU IN LONDON

Founded in 1865, Notre Dame de France was bombed during the Second World War. Reconstructed in the 1950s, the cultural attaché to the French Embassy in London imagined the church as a monument to the finest French art of the time, and invited Jean Cocteau, then painting at the Fishermen's Chapel in Villefranche. (An interesting choice, given that the first exhibition of Cocteau's work in London – at Peggy Guggenheim's Guggenheim Jeune gallery in 1938 – was nearly scuppered when his paintings were apprehended at Croydon Airport for their obscene suggestion of pubic hair.) Cocteau agreed to paint the Lady Chapel to the side of the church with scenes of the annunciation, crucifixion and assumption, but was asked to modify some of the male figures in his proposed scheme, thought by the priests to be too sensual. In November 1959, Cocteau spent eight days painting the work, starting each by lighting a candle to Our Lady of Lourdes. Wooden barricades had to be erected to keep television and news reporters at bay. Above his signature, Cocteau added the letters D.D.D – Delineavit, Dedicavit, Donavit – Drew, Consecrated, Given. The mural was inaugurated in 1960, and Cocteau offered the preparatory sketches to Princess Margaret.

# IDA KAR

The photographer celebrated for her portrayal of London's post-war bohemia had, herself, a life worthy of a three-volume novel. Born Ida Karamian to Armenian parents living in Tambor, Russia, her childhood was spent on the move, first to Iran, then Alexandria, Egypt. She moved to Paris in 1928, supposedly for a medical degree, but the lure of music and the avant-garde was overwhelming, and she fell into photography by way of surrealism. Her first photography studio was in Cairo with her husband Edmond Belali in the late 1930s. They exhibited with the Egyptian surrealists, but in 1944 Kar fell in love with British poet and art dealer Victor Musgrave, then serving in the RAF, and moved to London with him as the war ended. Through her surrealist contacts, and Musgrove's Gallery One in Litchfield Street, Soho, Kar started to photograph the artists of her new home city. In 1956 legendary dealer John Kasmin took his first artworld job with Gallery One, becoming both Kar's assistant and her lover (neither the first nor the last). In 1960, a solo exhibition of her photographs was held at Whitechapel Gallery; unprecedented in a time when photography was yet to be accepted as an artform.

## THE SEVEN NOSES OF SOHO
Various locations

In 1997, as CCTV became more prevalent, Rick Buckley fixed casts of his nose to sites around London, 'under the nose' of state surveillance. Of the purported 35 installed, most were detected and removed. One remains at Admiralty Arch off Trafalgar Square. A further six have been spotted around Soho. Buckley only claimed responsibility in 2011, by which time they had generated a whole subgenre of London mythology.

## EDUARDO PAOLOZZI'S TOTTENHAM COURT MOSAICS
Oxford Street, WC1A 1DD

There are sculptures by Paolozzi all around London, including the figure of Isaac Newton outside the British Library. The mosaics installed at Tottenham Court Road underground station relate more closely to his printed and tapestry works, linking the 'high' culture associated with the British Museum to images connected to the popular culture of Soho, such as cameras and saxophones. Commissioned in 1979, the project was completed in 1986, with different sections of the 950 square-metre design 'signed' and dated as Paolozzi completed them.

## LOUISE VINES,
### *ODE TO THE WEST WIND* (1989)
17 Noel Street, W1F 8GB

Poet Percy Bysshe Shelley lived for a while at 15 Poland Street. Shelley's *Ode to the West Wind* (1819) called out the 'Wild Spirit, which art moving everywhere; Destroyer and Preserver.' While honouring Shelley, Vine's mural, with its split tree trunk, commemorates the Great Storm of 1987, which destroyed 15 million trees.

## JULIAN OPIE,
### *SHAIDA WALKING* (2015)
Corner of Broadwick Street
and Carnaby Street

To capture the motion for this LED work, Opie invited people to walk on a treadmill, filming them at 50 frames per second. This realistic gait was re-drawn as a pared-down line animation that recalls the aesthetic of public information signage.

# COVENT GARDEN

## INSTITUTIONS

### THE COURTAULD GALLERY
Somerset House
Strand, WC2R 0RN
courtauld.ac.uk

Founded in 1930 by three eminent art collectors, the Courtauld Institute was London's first academic centre devoted to the history of art. Notable directors include art historian Anthony Blunt, who oversaw the Courtauld's flourishing between the 1950s and 1970s. (Blunt's Marxist beliefs were well known, but only on his retirement in 1974 was it revealed he had spied for the Soviet Union during the Second World War.) The Gallery houses Post-Impressionist works donated by Roger Fry, as well as Renaissance drawings and Impressionist masterpieces. Closed until 2021.

### KOREAN CULTURAL CENTRE
Grand Buildings, 1-3 Strand, WC2N 5BW
london.korean-culture.org

Covering matters cultural from K-pop to the cinema of Park Ki-Yong, this space on the Strand stages regular exhibitions of contemporary art from Korea, and has a free talks and discussions strand. Free.

### SOMERSET HOUSE
Somerset House, Strand, WC2R 1LA
somersethouse.org.uk

Magnificent palace stretching from The Strand to The Embankment, hosting exhibitions large (touring shows of art and fashion) and small (showcase displays by artists in residence) as well as an annual program of art fairs and special events. Special exhibitions ticketed.

### STORE X
180 The Strand, WC2R 1EA
180thestrand.com

Brutalist office block taken over by The Vinyl Factory – an art, music and arty music outfit launched by culturally attuned property developers. The raw spaces here host outstanding exhibitions – largely of audio-visual art – interspersed with pop-up events linked to film and fashion brands. Free.

# SOMERSET HOUSE

The first palace on this site was built for the Duke of Somerset in the sixteenth century. Centuries of expansion and restructuring followed, including stints overseen by Inigo Jones and Sir Christopher Wren, but by 1775 the building was in such a state that it was pulled down. The first section of the new building – the North Wing, occupied since 1989 by the Courtauld Gallery – was home to the Royal Academy of Arts between 1779 and 1837. For the next 150 years, most of Somerset House was occupied by the Inland Revenue, a presence that has progressively been exorcised as the building has transformed into a creative hub. Currently, it houses 250 creative organisations and resident artists, alongside its program of art, photography and fashion exhibitions. Annual fixtures include Photo London (May) and the 1–54 Contemporary African Art Fair (October). There are cafes and bookshops on site, and the courtyard hosts concerts and open-air screenings in the summer and a skating rink in the winter.

# ST. MARTIN'S SCHOOL OF ART

Founded in 1854 by the Reverent M. Mackenzie, education campaigner and vicar of St Martin-in-the-Fields, in its early years the art school occupied rooms within the church itself. The school moved to various sites before establishing itself on Charing Cross Road in 1913. During the 1960s and 70s, St Martin's was seen as London's leading art school, and its sculpture department, headed by Anthony Caro, held sway over a dynamic new generation of British sculptors. In 1989 it merged with Central to form Central St Martins.

## TWO TEMPLE PLACE
Two Temple Place, WC2R 3BD
twotempleplace.org

Built for shipping heir William Waldorf Astor in 1895, this lavishly decorated neo-Gothic palace was intended to be the great man's estate office (his other homes included Hever Castle in Kent and Cliveden in Buckinghamshire). No centimetre of the interior lies undecorated, from the intricate woodwork to the stained-glass windows. Closed for most of the year, Two Temple Place opens January to April for exhibitions of works from British regional collections. Ticketed.

# PUBLIC ART

## SHIRAZEH HOUSHIARY AND PIP HORNE, *EAST WINDOW* (2008) AND *ALTAR* (2011)
St Martin-in-the-Fields, Trafalgar Square, Charing Cross, WC2N 4JJ

St Martin-in-the-Fields has a long and close association with London's artists. Ahead of recent renovation, the church commissioned stark and dramatic new windows inspired by the story of Jacob's Ladder, installed above a new altar formed from a floating block of travertine limestone.

Shirazeh Houshiary's *East Window* (2008), St Martin-in-the-Fields Church

# COVENT GARDEN IN THE EIGHTEENTH CENTURY

'It was a magnet for every man of talent newly come to London,' wrote Vic Gatrell in *The First Bohemians* (2013), his spirited history of Covent Garden. 'It was full of artists, engravers, writers, dramatists, actors and advanced designers…Each of these regarded it "as the school of manners and an epitome of the world."' London was big, by city standards of the day, and Covent Garden piazza was its heart, surrounded by narrow alleys and rickety courtyards where human life throbbed in pungent concentration. At the Rose Tavern on Drury Lane, at Tom and Moll King's or the Bedford Coffee House could be found stimulating company, debate and the exchange of ideas, as well as female company, for a price. For the many artists who found an audience for erotic subjects – or those simply in need of a female model – local brothels provided a steady supply of young women. Skilled engravers worked with artists to create affordable multiples of their work; it was through these, rather than the sale of costly oil paintings, that many artists of the day supported themselves. The Royal Academy was dedicated to art in the lofty and heroic vein, vocally opposed to work in the Dutch realist tradition. By contrast, William Hogarth, Thomas Rowlandson, John Collet and the merciless caricaturist James Gillray were interested in depicting life as they saw it around them in Covent Garden – crime, corruption, drunkenness and squalor, yes, but also love, merriment and vivid scenes of real life.

# ANGELICA KAUFFMAN

Born in Chur, Switzerland, in 1741, Angelica Kauffman only lived in London for 15 years, but acquired immense status as an artist. One of two female founder members of the Royal Academy in 1768, Kauffman's chosen fields were history painting – unusual, and challenging for a woman in an era when study of the nude was not available – and portraiture. A great friend of Sir Joshua Reynolds, the two artists painted reciprocal portraits, and their relationship was the subject of some innuendo. In 1775 she attempted to block the exhibition of *The Conjuror*, a satirical work by Nathaniel Hone, which apparently featured a naked caricature of Kaufman behind a depiction of Reynolds (the young girl posed attentively at Reynold's knee is also thought an allusion to their 18-year age difference). In 1778, Kauffman was commissioned by the Royal Academy to paint four female figures – *Invention*, *Composition*, *Design* and *Colour* – embodying theories Reynolds set out in his *Discourses on Art*. The paintings were transferred with the Royal Academy when it moved to Burlington House, and displayed in the ceiling of the entrance hall. It has been suggested that the figures contained an element of self-portraiture.

# NICE STYLE: THE WORLD'S FIRST POSE BAND

'Creases, cuffs and collars. It was the three C's,' joked Bruce McLean, explaining the priorities of Nice Style, which first performed as support for The Kinks in 1971. Founded by St Martin's alumnus McLean, with Paul Richards, Ron Carr, Gary Chitty and Robin Fletcher (then his students at Maidstone College in Kent), Nice Style was a glam rock band re-imagined as sculpture. 'The whole visual imagery of rock music was inspiring to us, if not more inspiring than contemporary art at the time,' Chitty explained. Reintroducing the human figure to sculpture in a period dominated by abstraction, Nice Style was an exploration of advertising, pose and surface. They rented an office off The Strand, and publicised performances with posters and cards. The band's title and works echoed the aspirational advertising language of the time ('British Airways: The World's Favourite Airline'). 'Rock music was able to communicate feelings and express the ideas of the collective imagination in a way that visual art or sculpture couldn't,' Richards said. Concerned that costumes were pulling focus from their poses, Nice Style swapped their glam rock image for tuxedos, but split in 1975. Performance art was being taught in art schools; their gesture lost its radical edge.

# LAURA KNIGHT ON DRURY LANE

Dame Laura Knight's two best-known works were made many hundreds of miles apart, both far from London. The remarkable *Self Portrait* (1913), painted in the artists' community of Newlyn in Cornwall, shows the artist engaged in a nude study of her friend Ella Naper. It caused a scandal when presented to the Royal Academy (at the time it was rejected as 'vulgar'). Thirty-three years later, *The Nuremberg Trial* (1946) shows the Nazis – among them Goering, Hess and Speer – flanked by rows of black-clad lawyers and white-helmeted guards. Behind them, the city is pictured in rubble and flames. Born in Derbyshire in 1877, Knight's early life was marked by bereavement and poverty; she enrolled in Nottingham School of Art aged 13. Moving to London at the end of the First World War, Knight immersed herself in the ballet world. Gaining access her male peers could not, she produced intimate paintings of dancers in states of undress and contemplative unpreparedness. In 1936 she became the first woman elected to the Royal Academy since 1768. Between 1903 and her death in 1970, Knight showed 284 works at the Royal Academy, exhibiting in all but two years out of the 67.

# HOLBORN

## INSTITUTIONS

### BRITISH MUSEUM
Great Russell Street, WC1B 3DG
britishmuseum.org

Vast and exquisite collection of artefacts of international (and, in some instances, controversial) origin. Temporary shows range from surveys of world cultures, to displays themed around ideas of faith or dissent, to handsome art exhibitions. The museum today occupies a vast and tangled site, including state-of-the-art subterranean facilities for treating and caring for their extraordinary collection. Displays free, exhibitions ticketed.

### THE FOUNDLING MUSEUM
40 Brunswick Square, WC1N 1AZ
foundlingmuseum.org.uk

Founded by Thomas Coram in 1739, the Foundling Hospital looked after children at risk of abandonment. William Hogarth and composer George Frideric Handel helped turn it into a fashionable cause; Hogarth encouraged his contemporaries to donate works, creating in the process London's first public art gallery. The Foundling Hospital closed in 1954, and the Museum tells the story of the hospital and its public museum. It still has artist 'Fellows', and commissions and shows contemporary art.

### THE SOANE MUSEUM
13 Lincoln's Inn Fields, WC2A 3BP
soane.org

Architect Sir John Soane is survived by his designs for the Bank of England and Dulwich Picture Gallery, as well as his home at Lincoln's Inn Fields, for which he knocked down three existing buildings. He had the house and his collection preserved for the nation by an act of parliament in 1833. Highlights include Hogarth's *A Rake's Progress* (1733), works by Turner and Canaletto, and fabulous classical statuary, but the building is better considered as a total work of art, with Soane's use of mirrors and coloured glass adding to the atmospherics.

# COMMERCIAL GALLERIES

**HERALD STREET**
43 Museum Street, WC1A 1LY
heraldst.com

A central off-shoot for Bethnal Green's Herald Street, occupying a pretty Georgian townhouse; fitting for a gallery representing Pablo Bronstein, an artist fascinated by the legacy of Georgian architecture and its ersatz manifestations on the British high street. Gallery bedfellows include Michael Dean, Matthew Darbyshire, Amalia Pica, Alexandra Bircken and Lesley Vance.

# ISAAC JULIEN AND *VAGABONDIA*

Julien can summon up breathtaking images. Whether it's embracing lovers licked by the morning light in his homage to the Harlem Renaissance, *Looking for Langston* (1989), or Maggie Cheung as the airborne goddess Mazu in *Ten Thousand Waves* (2014), he can seduce viewers with sublime beauty, but that's only ever the surface. This artist's poetic vision serves his exploration of capital: the movement of money, and the movement of people and things in pursuit of it, from historic wealth built on enslaved labour, to contemporary migrant workers drowned picking cockles off the English coast. Many of Julien's works are projected on multiple screens, surrounding you in image and sound, so that impressions flood faster than you can process them. His two-screen work *Vagabondia* (2000) is set in The Soane Museum, bringing to life an overlooked character – a Black vagabond – from Hogarth's *A Rake's Progress*. Filmed at night, the house is repopulated by figures in historic dress, who perform against a voice-over in Saint Lucian Creole French provided by the artist's mother. The film is shot to reflect Soane's interest in mirrors, doubling and perspectival tricks in his architecture, but also suggests the origins of the wealth the house was built with.

# BLOOMSBURY

## INSTITUTIONS

### ART GALLERY AT UCL
University College London, Gower St,
King's Cross, WC1E 6BT
AND
Flaxman Gallery, King's Cross, WC1E 6BS
ucl.ac.uk/culture

University College London's collection has works dating back to the mid fifteenth century, as well as prize-winning paintings by students at the Slade School of Art, among them Stanley Spencer, Augustus John, Edward Wadsworth and Paula Rego. Prints and drawings from important bequests are shown in the print room. The Flaxman Gallery shows the contents of neoclassical sculptor John Flaxman's studio – including drawings and plaster models. Free.

### ARTS CATALYST
74-76 Cromer Street, WC1H 8DR
artscatalyst.org

Non-profit supporting the intersection of art, science and technology. Their track record is long and impressive, stretching back some 25 years over projects with Tomás Saraceno, Tania Bruguera, Helen Chadwick, Aleksandra Mir and dozens more. Itinerant until 2016, the little Bloomsbury site is both exhibition space and headquarters for Art Catalyst's projects around the country. Free.

### BRUNEI GALLERY
SOAS, Thornhaugh Street,
Russell Square, WC1H 0XG
soas.ac.uk/gallery

The School of Oriental and African Studies' Brunei Gallery shows work from Africa, Asia and the Middle East, often the fruit of research projects, and with an acute awareness of the political context in which it is made and is shown. The Japanese roof garden, planted with lemon thyme and wisteria, is used for performances, exhibitions and tea ceremonies.

### THE PERIMETER
20 Bronlow Mews, WC1N 2LE
theperimeter.co.uk

Private collection of contemporary art, housed in a Georgian mews building converted by 6a Architects. The changing display is drawn from a collection that includes works by Phyllida Barlow, Taryn Simon, Sarah Lucas, Eva Rothschild and Wilhelm Sasnal. Visits for a maximum

# GWEN JOHN AND THE WOMEN OF THE SLADE SCHOOL

Opened in 1871, the Slade School of Art had a progressive reputation, welcoming female students with equal status, including study of the nude – a privilege not extended at the Royal Academy Schools until 1903. The Slade attracted female artists looking to establish a serious career, among them, in the 1890s, a group of remarkable talents: Edna Clarke Hall, Gwen John, Ida Nettleship and Gwen Smith. Clark Hall (then Waugh) was only 14 when she enrolled in 1893. Biographer Alison Thomas recounts her interview with drawing master Henry Tonks, who, leafing through the romantic sketches in her application, suggested she aspired to be a second Burne-Jones. 'No, the first Edna Waugh!' came her sharp reply. Gwen John joined in 1895, at the urging of her brother Augustus. The four women's time at the Slade was happy and productive. They enjoyed visits to Sadler's Wells music hall and intense work sessions during which they sat for one another. The shared purpose, camaraderie and focus of these years was something they would struggle to achieve again. Nettleship married Augustus John soon after leaving the Slade, and had five children in quick succession. Parenthood did little to modify Augustus's lifestyle. In 1903, after Ida had her second son, he became obsessed with Dorothy McNeill, known as Dorelia. In 1905, all three – accompanied by five young children: Ida's four and Dorelia's first – moved to Paris together. Ida died in 1907, shortly after delivering a fifth son. For both Edna Clark Hall and Gwen Smith, marriage and motherhood made painting difficult. Clark Hall, married to a champion of children's rights, felt crushed by her husband's lack of interest. Gwen Smith, by contrast, put her creative needs second to those of her husband, Matthew Smith, raising their children alone. Gwen John moved to Paris soon after leaving the Slade. Early on she supported herself as an artist's model – most famously for Auguste Rodin, with whom she had a short but affecting love affair. She dedicated herself to art with fiery intensity, often enduring great poverty – alleviated, gloriously, in 1910 when American collector John Quinn stepped in as her patron. 'If I had to make a choice between the painting by you…and the Picasso, I should cheerfully sacrifice the Picasso', he once told her. Thus supported, she flourished and her beautifully observed, delicately assured paintings were regularly shown at the Parisian 'Salons'. Quinn died in 1924, and John became insular, focussing on her work and her Catholic faith, subsisting for her final years on milk and ground barley.

# THE BLOOMSBURY GROUP

In October of 1904, the younger members of the Stephens family – writer Virginia, artist Vanessa and their brother Thoby – moved from the grand gloom of Hyde Park to 46 Gordon Square in less reputable Bloomsbury. Virginia, convalescing after a breakdown, thought it 'the most beautiful, the most exciting, the most romantic place in the world'. Thoby drew around him friends from his student days, among them writers Lytton Strachey, Clive Bell and Leonard Woolf (who many years later would marry Virginia), and the artist and critic Roger Fry. Thursday night salons held by the siblings at Gordon Square established the kernel of what later became know as the Bloomsbury Group. Progressive in life as in ideas, they were compelled by pursuits of the heart and head alike; not for nothing is Amy Licence's biography titled *Living in Squares, Loving in Triangles*. Thoby died of Malaria in 1906, but the social and intellectual ties drawn around him remained. Vanessa married his friend Clive Bell in 1907. The previous year, she had started a Friday group for artists, and a play-reading club took the place of Thoby's Thursday meetings. Vanessa later recalled that the talk was of 'anything that came into our heads'. Openness and emotional honesty were prized, as was directness and familiarity. ('Semen?' Strachey once enquired, noticing a stain on Vanessa's dress.) In 1910, as he prepared for London's first exhibition of Post-Impressionist art, Roger Fry wrote to his occasional lover Ottoline Morrell: 'I am preparing for a huge campaign of outraged British Philistinism.' The huge exhibition featured works by van Gogh, Cézanne, Gauguin and Matisse. Critical response was indeed outraged: the man from *The Daily Telegraph* reportedly threw down his catalogue and stamped on it. Naturally, huge crowds followed. For Vanessa Bell, Duncan Grant and others of their generation, it was revelatory. Their work was included in Fry's second Post-Impressionist exhibition – held in 1912 – alongside that of Stanley Spencer, Wyndham Lewis, Spencer Gore and Eric Gill. The following year, Fry established the Omega Workshops, an enterprise dedicated to the decorative arts. With the hell of war, Bloomsbury sought sanctuary in the countryside. There were inebriate and sexually-charged visits to Ottoline Morrell's decadent Garsington Manor in Oxfordshire in the company of the great writers, artists and intellectuals. And more permanent moves: Strachey and Dora Carrington shifted rural, as did the evolving ménage clustered around Vanessa and Clive Bell and Duncan Grant. The Woolfs had already decamped to Hogarth House in Richmond, from which they founded the Hogarth Press, the imprint that issued many of Virginia's novels.

# JOHN EVERETT MILLAIS

So prodigious was Millais's talent that his family moved from Southampton to Gower Street in 1838 so that their nine-year-old son could receive instruction. Aged 11, he was admitted to the Royal Academy Schools; aged 17, he showed *Pizarro Seizing the Inca of Peru* in the annual exhibition. Part of the Pre-Raphaelite Brotherhood, it was Millais's *Christ in the House of His Parents* (1849-50) that was the particular focus of critical attacks. Millais had been inspired by the writing of John Ruskin, and Ruskin championed him in return, commissioning a portrait magisterially positioned in front of the waterfall at Glenfinlas. Long before this trip to Scotland, Millais conceived a fascination for Effie Gray, Ruskin's unhappy wife. Effie's Perthshire background provided an excuse for her to model as the wife of a Jacobite rebel for *The Order of Release 1746* (1852-3), an unconventional undertaking for a married woman. The painting caused a sensation at the Royal Academy, and a policeman was installed in front to keep the crowd moving. The Ruskins' unconsummated marriage was annulled, and Effie and Millais married in 1855, settling in Perth. Shortly before his death, Millais was elected President of the Royal Academy; an immaculate arc from rebel to the acme of the establishment.

# THE REBEL ARTS CENTRE

38 Great Ormond Street was headquarters to the Futurist-inflected Vorticist group that split from the Omega Workshops in 1913; among them Wyndham Lewis, Henri Gaudier-Brzeska, Edward Wadsworth and Kate Lechmere. Decorated with murals by Lewis and screens by Christopher Nevinson, it closed as war was declared in the summer of 1914. Both Wyndham Lewis and Gaudier-Brzeska enlisted to fight; the latter died at Neuville-Saint-Vaast the following June, aged 24.

of eight people are on Wednesdays and Thursdays, by appointment only. Free

## PETRIE MUSEUM
**University College London, Malet Place, WC1E 6BT**
ucl.ac.uk/culture/petrie-museum

UCL's collection of Egyptian and Sudanese Archaeology was based on a bequest by the nineteenth-century writer Amelia Edwards, and the work of professor William Flinders Petrie, who excavated dozens of major sites, donating his discoveries to the museum. One of the largest collections of Egyptian antiquities outside Egypt, it holds early pieces of linen and iron beads from the region, stone carvings, frescoes, mummy portraits, armour and papyrus documents. Free.

## WELLCOME COLLECTION
**183 Euston Road, NW1 2BE**
wellcomecollection.org

Endlessly fascinating and surprising (for what is more fascinating and surprising than our own bodies?), Henry Wellcome's titular collection is of ephemera artistic, spiritual, cultural and technical related to health, medicine and the human body. Beautifully mounted exhibitions use commissions from contemporary artists alongside historic artefacts to explore issues ranging from drugs, sleep and sex to the science of magic and perception. Free.

# COMMERCIAL GALLERIES

## GAGOSIAN BRITANNIA STREET
**6-24 Britannia Street**
**London WC1X 9JD**

The largest of Gagosian's three London sites occupies old brick-built industrial spaces just south of King's Cross. Renovated by Caruso St John, the 1,400 square-metre ground floor can take exhibitions on a monster scale, from Chris Burden's sculptures made with entire cars, to Richard Serra's curved and tilted steel, to Rachel Whiteread's massive interior casts.

## OCTOBER GALLERY
24 Old Gloucester Street, WC1N 3AL
octobergallery.co.uk

Founded in 1979, October promotes what it refers to as the transvangarde: art of the trans-cultural avant-garde. That cutting edge contemporary art from around the world includes work by El Anatsui, Kenji Yoshida, Brion Gysin and Aubrey Williams. October is a charitable trust, offering an education program sustained in part by exhibition sales.

## PUBLIC ART

**MARK WALLINGER,
THE WORLD TURNED UPSIDE
DOWN (2019)**
London School of Economics,
Sheffield Street, WC2A 2AP

A four-metre globe balanced on its north: 'This is the world as we know it from a different viewpoint,' says Wallinger. 'Familiar, strange, and subject to change.'

# WILLIAM HOLMAN HUNT AND THE AWAKENING CONSCIENCE

Born in Cheapside, the son of a warehouse manager, Holman Hunt worked as an office clerk before being accepted to the Royal Academy Schools in 1844. Here he met Millais and Rossetti, co-founders of the Pre-Raphaelite Brotherhood. Holman Hunt was to spend considerable time in the Holy Land, and even his early paintings are notable for their symbolism and religious themes. *The Awakening Conscience* (1853) shows a revelation occurring as a man sings with his mistress in the lodgings in which he has installed her. Rising from his lap she is surrounded by ominous signs of the situation she finds herself in: a cat toying with an injured bird, a discarded glove, and a tangle of yarn. Holman Hunt's on/off girlfriend Annie Miller was the model; she was much fought over amongst the Brotherhood, and he certainly had an urge to 'rescue' her, paying for her education during his first trip to the Holy Land in 1854, supposedly with a view to marriage on his return. Against Holman Hunt's wishes, Miller modelled for Rossetti during his absence (much to the fury, too, of Rossetti's girlfriend Elizabeth Siddal, who once threw his drawings of Miller out of the window).

# CLERKENWELL, FARRINGDON AND THE CITY

## INSTITUTIONS

**BARBICAN CENTRE**
Silk Street, EC2Y 8DS
barbican.org.uk

The arts centre in the labyrinthine Brutalist development has a program that extends from clowning workshops to avant-garde music. The free-to-enter Curve houses commissions on a massive scale, while the ticketed gallery on the second floor stages huge thematic exhibitions on art, fashion and design, with a focus on Modernism. Some of the most interesting programming in London, the shows tend to be intense and packed with ideas. Look out for Banksy's tribute to Jean-Michel Basquiat in the access tunnel.

**BETTS PROJECT**
100 Central Street, EC1V 8AJ
bettsproject.com

Architecture-focused gallery, exploring current ideas and presenting architectural objects as works of art. Free.

**GUILDHALL ART GALLERY**
Guildhall Yard, EC2V 5AE

Victorian gallery showing the art collection of the City of London, badly bomb-damaged during the Second World War. Art of the Victorian period and pictures of London remain the focus. In the 1980s, the remains of a Roman Amphitheatre were discovered beneath the building: they're now shown in an adjacent space.

**KUNSTRAUM**
21 Roscoe Street, EC1Y 8PT
kunstraum.org.uk

European-facing non-profit exhibition space with a strong line in performance and bookish events. Free.

**LONDON MITHRAEUM BLOOMBERG SPACE**
12 Walbrook, EC4N 8AA
londonmithraeum.com

Bloomberg's London headquarters sits over the lost River Walbrook, which marked the limits of Roman Londinium. In 1954, archaeologists discovered the remains of a temple to Mithras built in the third century CE. Temple and artefacts share space here with site-specific commissions.

# COMMERCIAL GALLERIES

**ARCADE**
87 Lever Street, EC1V 3RA
thisisarcade.art

Gallery on a small domestic scale; artists with big institution-facing ideas. Favourites include Caroline Achaintre, whose woven, rug-like wall works have been widely shown.

**BEERS**
1 Baldwin Street, EC1V 9NU
beerslondon.com

Founder Kurt Beers is author of *100 Painters of Tomorrow*, and unsurprisingly painters feature heavily in the list of artists here. He's also Canadian – hence that list features paint-smeared compatriots Kim Dorland, Kathryn MacNaughton, Andy Dixon, Andrew Salgado and Gord Bond.

**HOLLYBUSH GARDENS**
1-2 Warner Yard, EC1R 5EY
hollybushgardens.co.uk

Down the steps, beneath a bridge, up an alleyway, and, confusingly, still named after its old location in Bethnal Green, it's almost as if Hollybush Gardens doesn't want to be found. Persevere, because this little gallery has a fantastic track record, not least two recent Turner Prize winners: Lubaina Himid (in 2017) and Charlotte Prodger (in 2018.)

**MODERN ART**
4-8 Helmet Row, EC1V 3QJ
AND
50-58 Vyner Street, E2 9DQ
modernart.net

Modern Art stage impeccable shows across two handsome exhibition spaces (the other in Bethnal Green). Stuart Shave has built up a great list of artists over 20 years, among them sculptor Eva Rothschild, punk collagist Linder and photographer Collier Schorr.

# PUBLIC ART

**SCULPTURE IN THE CITY**
sculptureinthecity.org.uk

Brilliant enterprise positioning contemporary sculpture amid the alienating and impersonal towers of the financial district. Works and locations change annually but quality is high.

**ST BARTHOLOMEW'S HOSPITAL MUSEUM**
66 W Smithfield, EC1A 9DY
bartshealth.nhs.uk

St Bart's has been on this Smithfield site for almost 900 years. William Hogarth donated two huge works – *The Good Samaritan* (1737) and *Christ at the Pool of Bethesda* (1736) – painted on the staircase above the great hall.

# NORTH

# UP THE EDGWARE ROAD: ST JOHN'S WOOD AND MAIDA VALE

## INSTITUTIONS

**BEN URI**
108A Boundary Road
St John's Wood, NW8 0RH
benuri.org.uk

Founded in Whitechapel in 1915, amid a blossoming of Jewish creativity, Ben Uri was named for a biblical craftsman and founded to support the work of émigré artists. They have a fabulous collection – notably works by the Whitechapel Boys (and girls), including David Bomberg and Mark Gertler – but are currently housed in a cramped shopfront space while they search for new premises.

**THE SHOWROOM**
63 Penfold Street, NW8 8PQ
theshowroom.org

Big-hearted institution supporting artists local and global for over 30 years. The artists they've shown are sterling – among them Lawrence Abu Hamdan, Mona Hatoum, Jim Lambie, Uriel Orlow, Eva Rothschild, Simon Starling and Rebecca Warren – but they also give much-needed space to work less likely to thrive in commercial contexts.

## COMMERCIAL GALLERIES

**KÖNIG GALLERIE**
259 Old Marylebone Road, NW1 5RA
koeniggalerie.com

Subterranean London outpost for the irreverent Berlin gallery. Intellectual gameplay comes from Alicja Kwade, whose sculpture springs from ideas about science and the cosmos. Perceptual gameplay, courtesy Jeppe Hein, who has a disconcerting way with mirrors and motors. And the art world gameplay to end all gameplay from Elmgreen & Dragset, the artists behind Prada Marfa.

**LISSON GALLERY**
27 Bell Street, NW1 5BY
lissongallery.com

Founded in 1968 and still run by Nicholas Logsdail, Lisson is enduringly contemporary (if you can be such a thing). Occupying two buildings on Bell Street, the gallery represents top-ranking international artists, from Ai Weiwei and Anish Kapoor to Marina Abramović and John Akomfrah.

(Previous pages: Camden Arts Centre)

# NEW BRITISH SCULPTURE

By the late 1970s, British critics were actively bemoaning the parochialism of London's art scene; international collectors had little interest in the city. The market had become so turgid that the art magazine *Studio International* stopped publishing for a while, with editor Richard Cork explaining: 'Magazines such as *Studio* can only survive if there is a viable market for contemporary art, which regrettably, there is not really today in the UK.' Enter a generation of sculptors who stepped away from minimalism and conceptual art during the early 1980s to explore form and more traditional materials and techniques. A number started attracting attention (reviews and, god forbid, actual sales), among them Helen Chadwick, Tony Cragg, Richard Deacon, Susan Hiller, Shirazeh Houshiary, Anish Kapoor, Richard Wentworth, Alison Wilding and Bill Woodrow. Of these, a significant number – Cragg, Woodrow, Deacon, Kapoor, Wentworth and Houshiary – were represented by Lisson Gallery, with which New British Sculpture became indelibly associated. Critic Waldemar Januszczak even referred, in one review, to the 'Lisson Boys', and the gallery was certainly seen as a hot prospect by the subsequent generation of Young British Artists who emerged on their coat-tails at the end of the decade.

# THE ST JOHN'S WOOD CLIQUE

Formed in 1862, the artists of the St John's Wood Clique – among them George Adolphus Storey, Philip Calderon, George Dunlop Leslie, John E. Hodgson, W.F. Yeames, David Wilkie Wynfield and Henry Stacy Marks – shared a taste for drama, if not a unifying style. Together, they rented Hever Castle in Kent as a painting location, joined the Artists' Rifles for 'bloodless field days' and enjoyed social gathering where they costumed themselves as Old Master paintings. A second generation formed around Lawrence Alma Tadema. A meticulous painter of Egyptian and classical scenes, he paid no less attention to the design of his home at 17 Grove End Road (purchased from the French painter James Tissot). Moving into the house in 1883, Tadema reportedly spent £70,000 on the interiors, resulting in 'a studio of unusually large proportions, with a domed ceiling filled with amber glass,' as Alan Montgomery Eyre described it in 1913. 'The walls are panelled with grey-green Sienna marble, the apse and dome are covered with aluminium leaf; in the atrium leading from the studio the ceiling is a copy from one in Pompeii...From a balcony on a landing one overlooks a Roman scene, with its marble basin and playing fountain.'

# JO BROCKLEHURST DRAWS THE PUPPY COLLECTIVE

Over four decades Jo Brocklehurst painted the nocturnal life of London in all its peacock finery: cabaret artists, bohemians, New Romantics, punks, drag queens and fetish fans. Of Sri Lankan-British parentage, and remembered as an extraordinary beauty, Brocklehurst felt an outsider, and was drawn to liminal territory. In the 1960s, her interest in fashion illustration gave way to a fascination with club life. Dressed in black, with her face hidden behind sunglasses, she drew in situ: first in hashish-scented jazz dives and the strip joints of Soho; later at the Blitz club, where London's New Romantics took pains to outdo one another. At the dawn of the 1980s she befriended the punk Puppy Collective who had squatted a building near her studio. Brocklehurst persuaded them to sit for her: singly, in pairs, and in various states of undress. Siouxsie Sioux and Billy Idol appear alongside a host of bright-haired rebels, many indifferent to the confines of gender. She had a horror of being pigeonholed by anything so irrelevant as age; from the early 1990s, Brocklehurst's public appearances were undertaken in a bobbed blonde wig, with a number of pairs of outsized sunglasses stacked up her forehead, shielding her face from view.

Hettie Judah © 2017 The New York Times

# LEON KOSSOFF

Raw, foundational, things that show you their workings whether it be paintings or parts of a city – that's what interests Leon Kossoff. Born to a Ukrainian-Jewish family in the East End, and one of seven children, Kossoff grew up in a house where art had no place. Somehow, in 1936, at the age of ten, he stepped into the National Gallery. He had never seen a painting before; 'they scared me', he told Jackie Wullschläger, in an interview in the *Financial Times*. By then, aged 87, he was permitted to enter the galleries before opening hours to draw uninterrupted, working the pictures apart, taking them, too, back to something raw and foundational. He had not always been so welcome in the gallery: 'When I met Frank [Auerbach], we used to go together. His drawings were marvellous and bold, I learnt from him to be bolder. Then I got too bold and for a while I wasn't allowed to draw here because I made too much mess on the floor.' Living in Kilburn since the 1960s, he has captured the workings of the changing neighbourhood over the years – train stations, swimming pools, dirty streets, close friends and family.

# KILBURN AND KENSAL

## INSTITUTIONS

**LONDON PRINT STUDIO**
425 Harrow Road, W10 4RE
londonprintstudio.org.uk

Long-established artist-run printmaking studio and gallery. Excellent public courses and a lovely little shop selling affordable artist prints. The space is run by John Phillips, who founded the studio in 1974 as a poster-making centre for the community.

**KINGSGATE PROJECT SPACE**
110-116 Kingsgate Road, NW6 2JG
kingsgateworkshops.org.uk

Small gallery space attached to the Kingsgate artist workshops, showing historically engaged exhibitions and surprising contemporary group shows.

## SCOTTIE WILSON

'Scottie' was a nod to Glasgow, but who knows where 'Wilson' came from; he was born Louis Freeman and grew up unlettered, joining the army at 16. His early career was chequered: funfairs, circuses, junk dealing, periods in Ireland and Canada. Scottie started drawing at the back of his shop in Toronto at the age of 40, making complex compositions shaded with careful cross-hatching that drew in motifs of birds, swans, fish and stylised faces. All related to a personal symbolism structuring his worldview, including the House of Peace, House of Birds and House of Knowledge. Moving to London after the Second World War, he took rooms on Lynton Road in Kilburn, though seems not to have thought much of the area, describing it as 'a jungle and the people mostly cannibals.' Nevertheless, he stayed there until his death in 1972. His work sold well and was widely collected, but he stuck to an austere routine, structured around visits to the Lyons tea shop. 'Scottie is not a naïf, a primitive, or a Sunday painter,' wrote Victor Musgrave after his death. 'He is unique, and his work penetrates the depth of the psyche, a living illustration of the theories of Jung.'

# ISHBEL MYERSCOUGH
## Islington

Dedicated to meticulous observation from life, and scrupulous attention to the smallest detail – freckles, shadows, floating strands of hair – Ishbel Myerscough's paintings have a super-real intensity. The figures in her portraits are fiercely present, available, in their static state, for a scrutiny that our fuzzy impression of living figures rarely affords. Winner in 1995 of the BP Portrait Award, she has a number of commissioned portraits in the National Portrait Gallery, including those of the actress Helen Mirren and opera singer Willard White. The subjects she constantly returns to are herself, her close friends and her family. She charts the changes to her own face and body as the years pass and she goes through periods of grief and change. She is unsentimental in her observation both of her children and herself. 'The reality of the female experience shifts as we age, as we advance from little girls, to teenagers, maybe mothers and beyond,' she has said. 'This is also determined by how the world's opinions of womanhood shifts and what is projected onto women and girls of all ages. My paintings of female friends and family address the intimate reality of what this feels like.'

# HAMPSTEAD

## INSTITUTIONS

### 2 WILLOW ROAD
2 Willow Road
Hampstead, NW3 1TH
nationaltrust.org.uk/2-willow-road

The 1930s home of Ernö Goldfinger and his family is one of London's most important Modernist buildings (his neighbour Ian Fleming might not have agreed – he named James Bond's nemesis after the architect by way of thanks for ruining his view). The interior is very Bauhaus – smooth lines, bold colours, flexible spaces; it's beautifully designed for displaying art. Goldfinger's collection included small works by Eileen Agar, Henry Moore, Prunella Clough, Roland Penrose, and Goldfinger's wife Ursula Blackwell. Ticketed.

### BURGH HOUSE
New End Square, NW3 1LT
burghhouse.museumssites.com

Local museum in a historic house. The collection includes thousands of artworks and objects relating to Hampstead, including the second issue (of two) of the Vorticist publication *BLAST*.

### CAMDEN ARTS CENTRE
Arkwright Road, NW3 6DG
camdenartscentre.org

One of London's great mid-sized art institutions; ambitious solo shows of British and international artists, smaller displays of work created on residencies. They also do great arts courses for both adults and children. Nice café/garden/bookshop. Free.

### FENTON HOUSE
Hampstead Grove, NW3 6SP
nationaltrust.org.uk/fenton-house-and-garden

Late seventeenth-century house in a walled garden high up in Hampstead. The house was left to the National Trust in the 1950s, and much of the art dates from the preceding century, notably significant works by William Nicholson, as well as paintings by Laura Knight, Duncan Grant, G.F. Watts and Walter Sickert. Ticketed.

# FRANCIS NEWTON SOUZA AND YOUNG LADIES FROM BELSIZE PARK

Born in Goa in 1924, the Catholicism that came as part of that city's Portuguese heritage seeps everywhere into F.N. Souza's intense paintings. Souza arrived in Britain in 1949. After a few years of desperate poverty, his paintings started to be widely exhibited – and written about – in the mid 1950s. Working with a strong, expressionistic line and dark colour palette, Souza drew together Catholic themes, art historical references and elements of the London everyday. Describing his painting *Mr Sebastian* from the mid 1950s, Geeta Kapur notes that the painting 'takes after Saint Sebastian but wears a dark suit and the arrows that pierce the innocent body of the saint are here stuck into the man's face and neck with a vengeance which, judging from his evil countenance, he seems to merit.' Painted with heavy lines on a furious, fleshy background, Souza's brothel scene *Young Ladies from Belsize Park* draws directly from Picasso's *Les Demoiselles d'Avignon*; a pointed re-sampling of the great Spanish artist's own samplings from African art.

# DOROTHY BOHM

'Photographing in available light fascinated me and challenged me,' Dorothy Bohm said of the first time she photographed outside a studio. That was in 1947, during a trip to Paris. Bohm was bitten by the bug, and went on, over the next 70 years, to become one of the great chroniclers of London. Born in Königsberg, East Prussia (now Kaliningrad, Russia) in 1924, Bohm moved first to Lithuania, before being sent to school in England aged 15 to escape the Nazi threat. During the war, Bohm photographed Londoners needing a portrait to send to sons, grandsons and sweethearts at the front. By the late 1950s, she abandoned the studio altogether, dedicating herself to street photography. Following a major survey of her work alongside that of Don McCullin, Tony Ray-Jones and Enzo Ragazzini at the ICA in 1969, Bohm and curator Sue Davies established The Photographers' Gallery in 1971, with the aim of promoting and supporting photography as an artform. 'My fascination really, was to capture what the world was like,' she has said. 'I've always said I wanted to keep what would disappear. Because in my lifetime, I have seen all the things that have meant something to me disappear.'

## FREUD MUSEUM
20 Maresfield Gardens, NW3 5SX
freud.org.uk

The London home of Sigmund Freud and his child-psychoanalyst daughter Anna hosts art exhibitions inspired by the Freuds' life and work, or dealing with subjects of the mind. This has included site-specific shows by Mark Wallinger, Miroslaw Balka and Emma Talbot, and a special exhibition of work by Louise Bourgeois. Ticketed.

## KENWOOD HOUSE
Hampstead Lane, Highgate, NW3 7JR
english-heritage.org.uk

Kenwood House was lavishly remodelled by Robert Adam in the mid eighteenth century at the behest of William Murray, 1st Earl of Mansfield. It now houses a magnificent art collection donated by Edward Cecil Guinness in the 1920s, including significant works by Rembrandt, Vermeer, Reynolds, Gainsborough, Romney and Van Dyke. A painting from the original collection, showing Mansfield's mixed-race great niece Dido Belle, inspired the movie *Belle* (2013), much of which was set at Kenwood. The parkland is set with sculptural works by Henry Moore and Barbara Hepworth. Free.

Freud Museum, Hampstead

# JOHN CONSTABLE ON HAMPSTEAD HEATH

In 1827 Constable leased a house on Well Walk as an escape from city life. It was, he wrote to a friend, 'three miles from door to door' to his home on Charlotte Street. In Hampstead he could 'get always away from idle callers – and above all see nature – & unite a town & country life.' He had been making regular migrations to rural Hampstead since 1819, studying the landscape and cloud formations in every direction from an elevated vantage point above the Vale of Health pond. He called these cloud studies 'skying,' keeping detailed notes of the weather, time and wind direction that had produced them, explaining: 'No two days are alike, nor even two hours; neither were there ever two leaves of a tree alike since the creation of the world.' A controversial nominee to the Royal Academy in 1829, when he was already 53, this commitment to working up oil sketches in the open air set him apart from most of his contemporaries (with the notable exception, of course, of Turner). Nevertheless, Constable knew Hampstead Heath so well that by the end of his life he started elaborating it with imaginary windmills and rainbows.

# LEE MILLER AND ROLAND PENROSE

Leading figures within the British art scene before and after the Second World War, both Miller and Penrose had extraordinary portmanteau careers. Born in New York State in 1907, Miller was a sought-after fashion model but moved to Paris in 1929 where she effectively forced Man Ray to accept her as an assistant. Working closely, Miller and Man Ray developed the technique known as solarisation, and she started producing her own experimental photographs. After marriage in Cairo, she returned to Paris in 1937 where she met artist and writer Penrose, who had co-organised the International Surrealist Exhibition in London the previous year. Miller moved to London to be with Penrose in 1939, and the couple shared a home in Hampstead, amid a circle of artist friends. During the war Penrose taught camouflage techniques, shocking students with a photograph of Miller lying on a lawn naked but for camouflage netting. Miller commenced a new career as a photojournalist, documenting the blitz, and the horrors unfolding on the Continent for *Vogue* magazine. She was haunted by the atrocities she witnessed, and largely abandoned photography after the war, becoming, somewhat improbably, a celebrated experimental cook. In 1947 Penrose founded the ICA with critic Herbert Read.

# KING'S CROSS

## INSTITUTIONS

**BRITISH LIBRARY**
96 Euston Road, NW1 2DB
bl.uk

While you need a reader's card to access the Library's business end, the rest of the building (including desks, squashy work chairs and cafés) is open to the public. The gallery hosts exhibitions related to the printed word and works on paper, from Islamic calligraphy, to punk zines, comic books and Leonardo's notebooks. Major exhibitions ticketed.

**HOUSE OF ILLUSTRATION**
2 Granary Square
King's Cross, N1C 4BH
houseofillustration.org.uk

Small gallery dedicated to illustration and graphic works on paper, from Quentin Blake's delicious drawings for children to Sister Corita Kent's inspiring screen-prints. Ticketed.

**INSTITUTE OF PHYSICS**
37 Caledonian Road, N1 9BU
beta.iop.org

Swanky new King's Cross digs for the IOP include a freshly inaugurated exhibition gallery for sciencey art works. Free.

**LETHABY GALLERY**
1 Granary Square
King's Cross, N1C 4AA
arts.ac.uk

Exhibition space of the eminent Central St Martins School of Art and Design showing work by staff and alumni as well as current students. Free.

**PANGOLIN**
Kings Place, 90 York Way, N1 9AG
pangolinlondon.com

Sculpture gallery connected to the Pangolin Editions foundry, showing modern and contemporary works. Free.

# CAMDEN AND KENTISH TOWN

## INSTITUTIONS

### CRANFORD COLLECTION
PO Box 45588, NW1 4WW
cranfordarts.org

Displayed in a private house in Gloucester Gate, the Cranford Collection is based around works by female artists and British and German art from the 1980s and 90s. Think Rosemarie Trockel, Bridget Riley, Rebecca Warren, Rachel Harrison, Sarah Lucas, Lynda Benglis, Louise Bourgeois, Alice Neel, Albert Oehlen, Sigmar Polke, Martin Kippenberger and Gerhard Richter. The house reopened in 2019 following extensive renovations by David Chipperfield, expanding its exhibition space. Open to the public by appointment. Free.

### FREELANDS FOUNDATION
113 Regent's Park Road, NW1 8UR
freelandsfoundation.co.uk

Backed by Elizabeth Murdoch, the Freelands Foundation supports mid-career female artists, emerging artists, children's access to art, and the cultural institutions that help nurture them. They opened their own space in 2018 showing interesting new work in thematic group shows. Free.

### JEWISH MUSEUM
Raymond Burton House,
129-131 Albert Street, NW1 7NB
jewishmuseum.org.uk

Permanent display on Judaism, and Jews in Britain, and changing exhibition. Some on provocative themes (Blood! Money!); others on figures from the creative arts who happen to be Jewish, among them ceramic artist Lucy Rie and children's book legend Maurice Sendak. Ticketed.

### ROUND HOUSE
Chalk Farm Road, NW1 8EH
roundhouse.org.uk

Camden's nineteenth-century turntable engine shed has housed some momentous happenings and installations over the years, including the performance of Andy Warhol's play *PORK* (1971). It's still more of a gig and performance venue, but just occasionally will house a happening, or welcome in an installation.

# RASHEED ARAEEN

Over six decades, Rasheed Araeen has engaged with multiple traditions, curated ground-breaking exhibitions of overlooked work, offered a fearless critical voice as a writer, and provided a critical platform for other voices in the journals *Third Text* and *Black Phoenix*. He is, in other words, both a creator of work and of opportunities. Born in Karachi in 1935 and trained as a civil engineer, Araeen moved to London in 1964 in the hope that it would provide an inspiring and receptive forum. Here he developed participatory minimalist sculptures such as *Zero to Infinity* (1968) – latticed cube forms that could be moved and re-ordered by the audience. Working at the SPACE studios in St Katharine Docks, he created the performance action *Chakras* (1969), throwing coloured discs into the filthy water of the disused docklands. That year, Araeen won the prestigious John Moores Prize for sculpture; he credits the subsequent ambivalence of the British art establishment with catalysing a significant political turn in his work. Works such as the anti-racist performance *Paki Bastard* (1977) were unmistakably political in intent. Looking at the earlier generation of artists working in Britain, as well as his contemporaries, he identified the British art establishment's failure to accept work from multiple cultural perspectives within the story of post-war art. In 1989 he curated an exhibition, The Other Story: Afro-Asian Artists in Postwar Britain, at the Hayward Gallery as a gesture toward changing this imbalance. His inclusive art history, *The Whole Story: Art in Postwar Britain*, remains an ongoing project.

## ZABLUDOWICZ COLLECTION
176 Prince of Wales Road, NW5 3PT
zabludowiczcollection.com

This former Methodist chapel is the public-facing London incarnation of Anita and Poju Zabludowicz's redoubtable art collection, and is used as a carte-blanche space for invited artists in between exhibitions. Large-scale site-specific projects have ensued, involving VR, performance, and in one case a complete electrical takeover of the building. Free.

# COMMERCIAL GALLERIES

## THE COB GALLERY
205 Royal College Street, NW1 0SG
cobgallery.com

A plucky outlier from the commercial fray of central London, Cob is nurturing a fanbase within the city's fashion and performing arts crowds. They come for a menu of solo shows by gallery artists including Nina Mae Fowler, Robert Montgomery and Jason Shulman, interspersed with ideas-driven curated exhibitions, often with a feminist kick.

Zabludowicz Collection, Kentish Town

# GEORGIANA HOUGHTON

Abstract art? In 1860s London? Painted by a woman? Ah, but Georgina Houghton's wild spiralling watercolours were no mere artworks; they were a medium of communication with the spirit world, guided from the beyond. Born in 1814 in the Canary Islands, Houghton's family settled in Kentish Town, and Georgiana received training to become an artist. The loss of her beloved sister in 1851 led her to consult with a spirit medium. After attending her first séance in 1859, Houghton entered a three-month training period as a medium, and started spirit drawing in 1861. The first of Houghton's spirit guides was named Henry Lenny, a deaf-mute artist. Subsequent guides were more eminent, among them Titian and Correggio, though she soon selected a group named Zacharias, John and Joseph, with whom she produced drawings in watercolour and ink. Victorian London was enthralled by spiritualism and its artists were no exception; Dante Gabriel Rossetti held séances at his Chelsea studio after the death of his wife Elizabeth Siddal. In 1871, Houghton organised an exhibition at the New British Gallery on Old Bond Street, which nearly ruined her. Nevertheless, she continued with both her art and spiritualist practices until her death in 1884.

# KELPRA

In 1957, husband and wife Rose Kelly and Chris Prater set up the Kelpra screen-printing studio in Kentish Town. Chris, already a skilled printmaker, was enthralled by what might be achieved in the medium; starting with a tiny budget, working at their kitchen table with scraps of silk, Kelpra soon acquired an expert reputation. In 1959, they made their first artist print for Gordon House. Silkscreen was not considered an art medium, but it was impeccably suited to a generation engaged both with the torrent of images generated by advertising and popular culture, and the crisp precision of geometric abstraction. House sung Kelpra's praises, introducing Richard Hamilton, Eduardo Paolozzi and Joe Tilson to the studio. After Kelpra produced Hamilton's *Adonis in Y Fronts* (1963), he persuaded the ICA to sponsor a portfolio of prints. The list of participants now reads like a who's-who of the era, including Gillian Ayres, Peter Blake, Patrick Caulfield, David Hockney, Howard Hodgkin, Allen Jones, R.B. Kitaj, Victor Pasmore, Bridget Riley and William Turnbull. Kelpra's contribution to the art of the time was honoured in an exhibition at the Hayward Gallery; Prater later left his personal collection to Tate, laying the foundation of the museum's contemporary print collection.

# PAULA REGO

Rego's Camden Town studio performs as a stage for the artist's fantastical compositions. Here, she assembles props and models (often Lila Nunes, Rego's pictorial alter ego since 1985) in magic realist tableaux drawn from literature, folktales and her personal symbolic vocabulary. The effect is powerfully emotional; her *Dog Women* of the early 1990s evoke the enigmatic middle ground between cowering subservience and devoted loyalty. Her devastating *Abortion* series, made later that decade, draws on experience of backstreet abortions in 1950s London. Born in Lisbon, Portugal, in 1935, Rego was sent to Britain aged 16, and studied at the Slade School between 1952 and 56. There she met artist Victor Willing, then recently married. Living between Portugal and Camden, Rego and Willing eventually married in 1959, and moved to London full time in 1974. Much of Rego's work in the late 1980s captures complex emotions relating to her husband's ill health and increasing dependence: sturdy girls are shown ministering to pet dogs, or supporting powerless parent figures. In the revelatory documentary *Secrets & Stories* (2017), made by Rego's son Nick Willing, the artist describes her tricky marriage and struggle with depression, suggesting the work as a necessary sort of exorcism.

# FRANK AUERBACH

Auerbach has kept his subjects limited to a handful of regular models – among them his wife Julia, son Jake, and writers David Landau and William Feaver – and a few streets around him in Camden Town. 'This part of London is my world,' he has said. 'I've been wandering around these streets for so long that I've become attached to them and as fond of them as people are to their pets.' His work is informed by deepening understanding of these subtly changing forms, human and architectural, closely observed over decades. Born in Berlin in 1931, he came to London as a refugee aged eight. In the mid 1940s, while officially studying at Saint Martin's and the Royal College of Art, Auerbach started attending David Bomberg's subversive classes at Borough Polytechnic. Here he met and befriended Leon Kossoff, with whom his work shares affinities. His early paintings accrued thickly gnarled surfaces, the result of the artist each day painting over his work of the day before. Since the 1960s he has instead scraped down the surface afresh each day, with the final image the result of a single day's work built upon weeks of preparatory studies.

# SICKERT AND THE CAMDEN TOWN GROUP

An important British response to Post-Impressionism in the years before the First World War, the short-lived Camden Town Group formed around Walter Richard Sickert and Spencer Gore and drew on their down-at-heel neighbourhood for their closely observed paintings of contemporary life. A new London was emerging, shaped by electricity and the combustion engine. Beyond the sparkle and modernity, new social divides emerged alongside, and districts like Camden were becoming shabby and dilapidated. This is the world the Camden Town Group captured: underground and train stations, buses and cafes, cinemas and music halls, but also domestic interiors of the time. Sickert painted a series of sexually charged encounters: naked women lying on rumpled sheets in slim metal bedsteads with cold light filtering through back windows. One grouping – known as the *The Camden Town Murder* series – alludes to the killing of part-time prostitute Emily Dimmock in 1907. No doubt caught up in the sensational reporting of the event in his immediate neighbourhood, this was a world Sickert had already started exploring in works such as *Mornington Crescent Nude, Contre-Jour* (1907). Indeed, the titular work of the *Murder* series had originally simply been titled *What shall we do for the Rent?*

# BARRY FLANAGAN'S BOLLARDS

The 'science' of Pataphysics, playwright Alfred Jarry explained, 'will examine the laws governing exceptions, and will...describe a universe which can – and perhaps should be – envisaged in the place of the traditional one.' This law of exceptions guided Flanagan. In 1967, at a time when his tutors and contemporaries at Saint Martin's favoured sculpture in rigid metal, he worked instead with hessian, sand and rope, making works that were allowed to settle into their own shape and changed with each exhibition. In art as in life (if there was such a distinction): discovering the council planned to erect permanent bollards on the corner of Agar Grove near his house in Camden, Flanagan drove a truck armed with a cement mixer, industrial sewing machine and wheelbarrow up by night and stitched together large blue canvas sacks which were filled with a mix of sand and cement, placed around the street and fixed to the spot with length of rebar. Camden evidently forgave him: in 1980 they commissioned a public sculpture from Flanagan (this in sheet steel rather than sand and sacking). *Camdonian* is installed on Lincoln's Inn Fields and is popular with another generation of urban rebels as a skateboard ramp.

# ISLINGTON

## INSTITUTIONS

### CUBITT
8 Angel Mews, N1 9HH
cubittartists.org.uk

Down an alleyway off the Pentonville Road, artist-led organisation Cubitt supports emerging international artists and curators alike, with a gallery, studios and a taste for experimentation. Free.

### ESTORICK COLLECTION
39a Canonbury Square, N1 2AN
estorickcollection.com

Museum housing the late Eric and Salome Estorick's collection of early twentieth-century Italian art. Among the highlights: technologically inspired works by the Futurists, and works on paper by Modigliani and Morandi. Ticketed.

Estorick Collection, Islington

**FIVE YEARS**
Unit 2B1 Boothby Road
Archway, N19 4AJ
fiveyears.org.uk

Collaborative artists project showing work by its 12 participating members, each of whom organises two shows every 18 months. One show may contain the organising artist's own work, the other must not. Free.

**GEORGE PADMORE INSTITUTE**
76 Stroud Green Road,
Finsbury Park, N4 3EN
georgepadmoreinstitute.org

Occupying three floors above the legendary New Beacon Books store, the GPI houses archives relating to Black communities of Caribbean, African and Asian descent in Britain and continental Europe. Most date from between 1960-90, and there is a special section related to the arts, including the work of the Caribbean Artists Movement. Free.

# KESKIDEE CENTRE

Britain's first Black arts centre was founded in a converted Boys' Brigade mission hall on Gifford St in 1971 by architect Oscar Abrams and community activist Norma Ashe-Watt. Named for a bird native to Guyana, Trinidad and Tobago, Keskidee became a hub for culture, activism and education. While its most famous legacy is in theatre and music – Bob Marley shot the video for 'Is This Love' at Keskidee in 1978 – it was also an important home to the visual arts. In the early years it served as a meeting place for the Caribbean Artists Movement, members of which included cultural theorist Stuart Hall, sculptor Ronald Moody, painter Aubrey Williams, textile designer Althea McNish, and portraitist and illustrator Errol Lloyd. Lloyd was the centre's first artist in residence, followed by Nigerian artist-poet Emmanuel Taiwo Jegede, and Trinidad-born artist Caboo. In *Black Artists in British Art* (2014), artist historian Eddie Chambers records the formation of the Rainbow Art Group at Keskidee in 1978. Founded in response to the difficulty 'all ethnic minorities in the art world [...] find in getting their work considered seriously and supported through established channels,' it demonstrates Keskidee's essential position in providing studio and exhibition space for Black artists in London.

# PHYLLIDA BARLOW
## North London

Long an influential educator – at the Chelsea and Slade schools – for much of Phyllida Barlow's career, art making happened in a rather private way, out of sight in her studio. Then, as now, Barlow worked with unheroic materials associated with urban detritus: plaster, planks, scraps of cloth, paint, concrete. They related to the London she grew up in after the Second World War, when the broken buildings revealed their domestic insides through the scars of bomb damage. Barlow's sculptures often have a teetering aspect, threatening to collapse, fall, crush or rise up toward you through the weird perspectives she employs. In a matter of fact way, she often consigned her earlier work to a skip once shown; for one thing, she worked at scale, and she had nowhere to store it, for another, it seemed to fit the apparently ad hoc mood of her work. On her retirement from her role as Professor of Fine Art and Director of Undergraduate Studies at the Slade in 2009, her career as a sculptor underwent an almost miraculous blossoming of public interest: a solo show at Studio Voltaire in 2010 was followed immediately by a show at the Serpentine Gallery. The following year, she was elected a Royal Academician. In 2014, she received the prestigious commission to fill the Duveen Galleries at Tate Britain; in 2017 she represented Britain at the Venice Biennale. The 'miracle' that propelled Barlow's ascent over the last ten years was, finally, that of active attention being paid to the work of women artists of her generation. Barlow didn't change – the world changed.

## LUX
Waterlow Park Centre,
Dartmouth Park Hill
Highgate, N19 5JF
lux.org.uk

The location is cute – a cottage in the middle of Waterlow Park – but underestimate LUX at your peril. Evolved out of the London Film-Makers' Co-operative (a counterculture stalwart, founded in 1966), it has passed through multiple locations and incarnations in its 50+ years, but the core mission holds firm: supporting and promoting artists working with film and video. LUX's reach is international and they hold an astonishing archive; the gallery in the park is only the visible part of something much greater. Free.

## PARASOL UNIT
14 Wharf Road, N1 7RW
parasol-unit.org

Foundation led by art historian Ziba Ardalan, showing international artists overlooked or less known in the UK. That could mean a first UK show for a well-established artist such as Martin Puryear, or an emerging talent such as Tschabalala Self.

Lux, Islington

# COMMERCIAL GALLERIES

## J HAMMOND PROJECTS
Unit 2B2, Bomb Factory,
Boothby Road, N19 4AJ
jhammondprojects.com

Tucked into the unforgettably named Bomb Factory artist studio complex, Jennie and Justin Hammond's gallery hosts winningly idiosyncratic exhibitions, from Betty Tompkins's large paintings derived from pornographic close-ups, to the Beta Band archive. The Hammonds are part of the team behind cult art and footie mag *OOF*; hence their soccer-themed show Collective Failure.

## LARGE GLASS
392 Caledonian Road, Islington, N1 1DN
largeglass.co.uk

Masquerading as a glazier, and named in honour of conceptualist uberdaddy Marcel Duchamp (*The Bride Stripped Bare By Her Bachelors, Even* – aka *The Large Glass*). This modest-sized gallery in the unlikely quarters of Caledonian Road has a reputation for stimulating events and sparky dialogues between art and other things: psychoanalysis, labyrinth design, chairs.

## TINTYPE
107 Essex Road, N1 2SL
tintypegallery.com

Located in the former haberdashery shop Sew Fantastic, and next to taxidermists Get Stuffed, Tintype are understandably enamoured with their Essex Road location. As well as the usual menu of solo and group shows by the gallery's artists, they commission eight films inspired by Essex Road every autumn which are then back projected onto the gallery window during their winter shutdown. The summer recess is used as an opportunity for an artist to go wild in their window.

## VICTORIA MIRO ISLINGTON
16 Wharf Road, N1 7RW
victoria-miro.com
AND
14 George Street, Mayfair, W1S 1FH

Mega Islington outpost for the venerable and highly respected London gallerist. Miro's stable is full of major names – Grayson Perry, Isaac Julien, Yayoi Kusama, Alice Neel – and the shows across the three spaces in this gallery are museum sized.

WEST

# HYDE PARK AND KENSINGTON GARDENS

## INSTITUTIONS

**SERPENTINE AND SERPENTINE SACKLER GALLERY**
Kensington Gardens, W2 3XA;
Kensington Gardens, W2 2AR
serpentinegalleries.org

London's crucible of the avant-garde, helmed by legendary curator Hans Ulrich Obrist (catchphrase: 'URGENT!'). Serpentine's interests are mercurial: artificial intelligence; overlooked octogenarians; spirit mediums; fashion display; poetry; maps; and the future of work. Fundraising for all this is assisted by Serpentine's air of unstoppable cool (they even have their own Comme des Garçons perfume) embodied in a series of glamorous and forbiddingly exclusive summer parties. The result? Free, challenging shows across two park venues, and a café designed by Zaha Hadid.

**SERPENTINE PAVILION**
Kensington Gardens, W2 3XA

Since 2000, the Serpentine Pavilion's summer architecture commission has gone to architects of international standing yet to complete a project in the UK, among them Jean Nouvel, Frank Gehry, Peter Zumthor and Zaha Hadid. Open to the public and used by the gallery for performances and arty events.

## PUBLIC ART

**HENRY MOORE**
*ARCH (1980)*
Kensington Gardens, W2 2UH

This six-metre-high travertine arch was given to the nation by Henry Moore in 1980, two years after his eightieth birthday exhibition at Serpentine Gallery.

**G.F. WATTS**
*PHYSICAL ENERGY*
Kensington Gardens, W2 3XA

Onward! Progress! Watts's muscle-bound rider is all about forward propulsion, and the quest for new challenges; Watts worked on the composition on and off from 1883 until his death in 1904. While an earlier cast forms part of a memorial to Cecil Rhodes in Cape Town, this version was positioned in Kensington Gardens as a memorial to the artist himself in 1907.

Serpentine Gallery, Hyde Park

*Physical Energy* (1904), G.F. Watts, Kensington Gardens.
(Previous pages: Pitzhanger Manor, exhibition of work by Anish Kapoor (2019))

# LUCIE RIE

Born in Vienna in 1902, Lucie Rie was an acclaimed ceramicist by the time she fled Nazi Austria for London in 1938. During the war, she ran a ceramic button-making business out of her flat on Albion Mews, employing refugees. After the war, Rie found her delicately balanced, modernist-influenced style out of step with prevailing tastes in British studio pottery. With the help of Hans Coper (later an eminent ceramicist in his own right), Lucie Rie Pottery produced elegant tableware for the domestic market, sold at Heal's in London and Bonniers in New York. Rie pursued her own projects when time permitted. Her ambition was simply to earn enough to create on her own terms, making works that performed more as sculptural, architecturally engaged objects than functional vessels. Suggestive of modern living, her ceramics were shown at the Festival of Britain in 1951. From the 1950s until her death in 1995 she exhibited regularly, in Europe, North America and Japan as well as the Berkeley Gallery on Davies Street. Ceramic artist Edmund de Waal identifies a particular London sensibility: 'This sense of objects being part of a much larger world is what makes Rie and Coper stand out as urban potters, rather than potters alone. They both seemed to make their own accommodation with modernity. There was an affection for the city as a place to make, which sets them apart from the deep, English emotional investment in crafts in the country.'

# BELGRAVIA
# AND PIMLICO

## INSTITUTIONS

**CHELSEA SPACE**
16 John Islip Street, SW1P 4JU
chelseaspace.org

Public exhibition space within Chelsea College of Art, hosting shows by invited artists. Free.

**DELFINA FOUNDATION**
29/31 Catherine Place, SW1E 6DY
delfinafoundation.com

Delfina Entrecanales has supported London's artists since the late 1980s, first providing studios in East and South London, more recently opening a residency and studio space hosting artists from Asia and Africa. Seasons are clustered around a theme (food, public space, power…), reflected in the exhibition and events programs. Free.

**THE STUART
HALL LIBRARY**
16 John Islip Street, SW1P 4JU
iniva.org/library/

Founded by influential academic Stuart Hall in 1994, the Institute of International Visual Artists championed the cause of Black and Asian artists in the UK. Iniva has evolved to foster a new internationalism in art practices and to challenge established ideas of diversity and difference. The library is Iniva's 'critical and creative hub'– holding documents on art and artists from Africa, Asia and Latin America, and UK artists of African, Asian and Latin American heritage. Free.

**TATE BRITAIN**
Millbank, SW1P 4RG
tate.org.uk

Less attention grabbing (hence, less crowded) than its Modern sibling, Tate Britain is home to a mutable display of British art from 1500 to the present day, with Turner's bequest housed in its own wing. For half of each year, the grand central Duveen Galleries host a commission by a British sculptor; contemporary art is also honoured in the museum's Art Now displays. While most of the museum is free to enter, ticketed exhibitions are hosted in two large galleries, and take an open-minded view of how 'Britain' might be defined (van Gogh in Britain recently made the cut). The Rex Whistler restaurant downstairs is clad in the artist's much-loved mural *The Expedition in Pursuit of Rare Meats* (1927).

# THE PRE-RAPHAELITE BROTHERHOOD

The PRB was founded in September 1848 by painters Dante Gabriel Rossetti, William Holman Hunt, John Everett Millais, James Collinson and Frederic George Stephens, sculptor Thomas Woolner, and William Michael Rossetti, designated secretary. The latter Rossetti noted their aims thusly: '1, To have genuine ideas to express; 2, to study Nature attentively, so as to know how to express them; 3, to sympathise with what is direct and serious and heartfelt in previous art, to the exclusion of what is conventional and self-parading and learned by rote; and 4, and most indispensable of all, to produce thoroughly good pictures and statues.' Inspired by Italian painting of the fifteenth century, their work was distinguished by flattened perspective, strong outlines and intense, jewel-like colour. At the Royal Academy in 1850, Holman Hunt and Millais's works were singled out for attack, most blisteringly in Charles Dickens's appraisal of Millais's *Christ in the House of His Parents*: 'You behold the interior of a carpenter's shop. In the foreground of that carpenter's shop is a hideous, wry-necked, blubbering, red-headed boy, in a bed-gown [...] a kneeling woman so horrible in her ugliness, that (supposing it were possible for any human creature to exist for a moment with that dislocated throat) she would stand out from the rest of the company as a Monster, in the vilest cabaret in France or the lowest ginshop in England [...] Wherever it is possible to express ugliness of feature, limb, or attitude, you have it expressed.' As Oscar Wilde subsequently noted: 'In England, then as now, it was enough for a man to try and produce any serious beautiful work to lose all his rights as a citizen; and besides this, the pre-Raphaelite Brotherhood...had on their side three things that the English public never forgives: youth, power and enthusiasm.' Ruskin championed the PRB, and within a few years, they were causing a public sensation of a different kind. A second wave formed around Rossetti, Edward Burne-Jones and William Morris during the late 1850s.

# WILLIAM HOGARTH: THE PAINTER AND HIS PUG

In a period when the Royal Academy was exhorting art in the heroic vein – flattering, glorious, grand – Hogarth remained stubbornly devoted to real life. The drama, muck, and bawdiness of Covent Garden's coffee houses and taverns were Hogarth's territory. Joshua Reynolds and the Academy did not approve. 'The connoisseurs and I are at war, you know,' Hogarth explained to a young friend. Perhaps his art was more intimately bound up in the rapidly transforming city than any history painting could be: he made some of the first English theatre paintings, capturing John Gay's sensational *The Beggar's Opera* (1728); he engraved frontispieces for some of the earliest novels, Henry Fielding's *Tom Jones* (1749) and *Joseph Andrews* (1742). Like Reynolds, though, he was determined to make a case for English painting and promoted its public display, donating works to Saint Bartholomew's and Coram's Foundling Hospitals, that they might be seen by all. Printmaking was flourishing in London, as a growing middle class emerged with the wherewithal to purchase decorative luxuries for the home: engravings of Hogarth's popular 'moral' series *A Harlot's Progress* (1732), *A Rake's Progress* (1732–4), and *Marriage A-la-Mode* (1743–5) were sold on subscription. The 'moral' quality of such narrative works permitted the inclusion of compromising detail relating to the venal, sexual and alcoholic debauch of their protagonists, and one imagines Hogarth did so with wicked relish. 'The business of correcting the heart by chastising vice provided…alibis for the most eloquent improprieties,' as Vic Gatrell observes in *The First Bohemians* (2013). Hogarth's self-portrait with his beloved dog Trump, *The Painter and his Pug* (1745, on display at Tate Britain), beautifully encapsulates this balance between exquisite care and vulgar delight. Hogarth appears, in a portrait within a portrait, alert but insouciant, in a silk dressing gown and velvet cap. His oval canvas is propped up on volumes by great dramatic storytellers and wits: Shakespeare, Swift and Milton. To the left, his palette carries the 'line of beauty' – a serpentine curve that underpins his theory of aesthetics. To the right sits Trump, ears cocked lopsidedly, eyes cynically hangdog, tongue protruding lasciviously from his mouth. There's no fooling this dog. He sees everything, from the ground up.

# MIKE NELSON
## and *The Asset Strippers*

Working with complex, large-scale installations, Mike Nelson is a master of atmosphere, creating evocative scenarios that draw on specifics of time and place. His breakthrough *Coral Reef* was installed at Matt's Gallery in 2000, and subsequently shown at Tate Britain. A labyrinthine network of antechambers, each space promised access to something more substantial – a hostel or mini cab office – but led only to further waiting rooms, each infused with an unmistakable aura of dread. Inspired by science fiction novels – Stanislaw Lem's *Solaris* and *Roadside Picnic* by Boris and Arkady Strugatsky – Nelson mines the objects we surround ourselves with or that we reject for insight into the contemporary state. After representing Britain at the Venice Biennale in 2011, and in demand for site-specific works around the world, Nelson received the 2019 commission for the Duveen Galleries at Tate Britain. There, he presented *The Asset Strippers* – a barricaded installation housing monumental sculpture made from industrial components sold off by companies closing down or moving their manufacturing capability outside of Britain. Presented during a period of political instability, the work also related clearly to the twentieth-century sculpture shown in neighbouring galleries, much of it drawing on the evolving aesthetics of the machine age.

# KNIGHTSBRIDGE AND SOUTH KENSINGTON

## INSTITUTIONS

### BLYTH GALLERY
Level 5 Sherfield Building,
Imperial College, SW7 2AZ
imperial.ac.uk

Artist-run space attached to Imperial College, better known for work in science, engineering, business and medicine. Free

### DESIGN MUSEUM
224-238 Kensington High Street, W8 6AG
designmuseum.org

Housed in the former Commonwealth Institute – recently converted by John Pawson – the Design Museum's interests extend through fashion to tech, architecture, textiles and furniture. Ticketed.

### JAPAN HOUSE
101-111 Kensington High Street, W8 5SA
japanhouselondon.uk

Exhibitions at this recently opened Japanese Cultural Centre have covered colour theory, robots, paper and manga art. There's a strong program of events and technical demonstrations (sugar sculpture, anyone?) and an enthusiastically reviewed restaurant. Free.

### ROYAL COLLEGE OF ART
Kensington Gore, SW7 2EU
rca.ac.uk

One of three sites for the leading post-graduate art and design college, the Kensington campus houses architecture, design, fashion and curatorial courses. Degree shows – usually in the last week of June – offer a glimpse of where the world is going next. Free.

### ROYAL GEOGRAPHICAL SOCIETY
1 Kensington Gore, SW7 2AR
rgs.org

Extraordinary photographic exhibitions on geographical themes. Free.

### ROYAL SOCIETY OF SCULPTORS
Dora House, 108 Old Brompton Road, SW7 3RA
sculptors.org.uk

Long-established artist-led organisation in a beautiful listed building. Free exhibitions by sculptor members, as well as ticketed talks and workshops.

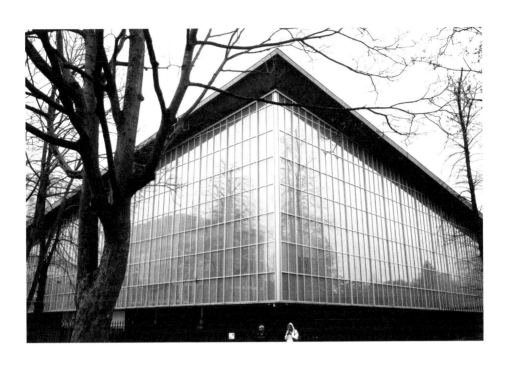

The Design Museum, inside and out

## VICTORIA & ALBERT MUSEUM
Cromwell Road, SW7 2RL
vam.ac.uk

The Museum of Manufactures opened on Pall Mall in 1852 under the directorship of Henry Cole, who notoriously schooled visitors with a cautionary display of 'bad design' in a Gallery of False Principles. It relocated to new buildings (gas-lit on winter evenings) at the current location in 1857. Expansions and improvements continued: in 1899, in the Queen's last public ceremony, the museum reopened as the Victoria & Albert, though work continued for a decade. Actually, it's barely stopped since: the most recent additions to this labyrinthine structure are a porcelain-tiled courtyard and subterranean galleries. A collection of art and design stretching back in time, and from around the world, is kept company by lavish exhibitions. The fashion blockbuster is a V&A staple, but it's not all Dior: recent shows have explored protest, food and designing for the future. Permanent displays free, exhibitions ticketed.

# JULIA MARGARET CAMERON

Born in Calcutta in 1815, and educated largely in France, Julia Margaret Cameron was introduced to photography by the astronomer Sir John Herschel in 1842. She commenced her photographic career aged 48 after she was given a camera by her daughter. Launching herself into the medium with formidable energy and great artistry, she produced affectionate works of portraiture and staged tableaux along mythic and religious themes. Her sitters for what she called 'fancy subjects for pictorial effect' were drawn from her family, household staff and her intellectual, bohemian circle. Using soft focus and dramatic lighting, and including imperfections such as streaks, swirls and even fingerprints in final prints, Cameron was criticised by some male contemporaries for her 'flawed' technique, though records of her working methods suggest the high degree of deliberation that went into her photographs, and the constant experimentation with new technique. In 1865, the South Kensington Museum (now the V&A) bought 114 of her photographs, which were put on exhibition. Three years later she was given two rooms in the museum to use as a portrait studio. Cameron and her husband moved to Ceylon – now Sri Lanka – in 1875 to be near their four sons. It is here she died in 1879.

# MADAME YEVONDE

Born Yevonde Cumbers Middleton in Streatham in 1893, Madame Yevonde was a portrait photographer, surrealist and pioneer of early colour photography who lived true to her motto: 'Be original or die'. Dispatched to a convent in Belgium as a teenager, Yevonde discovered the suffragette movement, and returned to London determined to forge an independent life. Aged 21, she set up studio as 'Madame Yevonde – Portrait Photographer', creating spirited portraits that evoked an era of increasing independence for women. Addressing the Professional Photographers' Association in the 1920s, she suggested women's sympathetic and intuitive nature made them better portrait photographers. In 1930, she became an enthusiastic convert to the new Vivex colour photographic process, presenting her groundbreaking colour photography at the Albany Gallery in 1932. The Gothic, moody and sensual *Goddesses* series followed: society women posed as classical figures in dramatic makeup and costume. Her colour studies of ship builders on the Clyde were included in 'Photography 1839-1937' at MoMA in New York. Vivex ceased production with the outbreak of war, bringing an end to Yevonde's experiments with colour. She continued working, and was honoured with a retrospective at the Royal Photographic Society on her eightieth birthday in 1973.

# DAVID HOCKNEY AT THE ROYAL COLLEGE OF ART

The London Hockney painted as a student, between 1959-62, is a far cry from the sun-smacked sensuality of his California years, or the sapid energy of his later Yorkshire landscapes. Within college walls, Hockney imbibed the paintings of Picasso, Pollock and Jean Dubuffet; beyond them, he learnt to read the surfaces of London as a young man entranced by suggestions of sex. The two worlds met in his paintings: the grubby chaos of inner city streets and lavatory walls scratched with graffiti form the basis of crude and vigorous pictures, ripe with innuendo. Hockney was smuggling codified messages into the paintings too. *We Two Boys Together Clinging* (1961) takes its title from a Walt Whitman poem, but also alludes to a newspaper headline that tickled him: 'Two Boys Cling to Cliff All Night.' The story was about a climbing accident, but Hockney had a crush on the pop star Cliff Richard at the time, and endowed it with quite another meaning. Hockney successfully lobbied the college for male life models, making his point in *Life Painting for a Diploma* (1962), in which he pasted a painting of a muscular-physique model over an earlier study of a skeleton.

# CHELSEA

## INSTITUTIONS

**SAATCHI GALLERY**
Duke of York's HQ, King's Road, SW3 4RY
saatchigallery.com

In the 1980s, the Saatchi Gallery was where you went to see the best contemporary art in London, amassed and displayed by the country's most significant collector. Those days have passed: artists have become wary of a collector who might dump their work on the market en masse, or refuse to lend to significant museums, and London is now rich in collectors and private foundations. The Saatchi in its Chelsea incarnation is a different beast: there are still collection shows, along more or less inflammatory themes, but also commercial tie-ins, hosted events and art fairs.

## COMMERCIAL GALLERIES

**MICHAEL HOPPEN**
3 Jubilee Place, SW3 3TD
michaelhoppengallery.com

Eminent photographic gallery staging diverse exhibitions, from Fergus Greer's portraits of Leigh Bowery to Gerry Cranham's sports photography, Daido Moriyama's Tokyo to the surreal fashion photography of Guy Bourdin.

**VIGO**
Saatchi Gallery, Duke of York's HQ,
King's Road, SW3 4RY
vigogallery.com

Somewhat nomadic gallery currently housed on the Saatchi premises. Vigo are particularly interested in artists of the African diaspora – notably the great modernist painter Ibrahim el-Salahi, and photographer Hassan Hajjaj's eye-catching works exploring consumerism, cultural clichés and Moroccan youth culture.

# DANTE GABRIEL ROSSETTI

Rossetti was torn between passions for poetry and art (and, notoriously, beautiful women). The son of an Italian writer and scholar, he grew up on Charlotte Street in Fitzrovia. Dante was a middle name, but he favoured its association with the great poet, whose work he translated, and whose *Divine Comedy* inspired his paintings. Medieval romance is where Rossetti found his principle inspiration: knights and maidens, fallen women, tragic love. In 1844, aged 16, he enrolled in the Royal Academy Schools. Encountering William Holman Hunt's *The Eve of St Agnes* (1848) – its subject drawn from a poem by Keats – he sensed kinship. He sought him out and, together with John Everett Millais, formulated the principles of the Pre-Raphaelite Brotherhood. Rejecting the mannered Grand Style of the Royal Academy, the PRB favoured close observation from nature, powerful emotion and intense colour reminiscent of fifteenth-century Italian art. Rossetti indiscreetly let slip the existence of the PRB (intended as a secret society) to a journalist on *The Times*. The revelation coincided with a deluge of mocking hostility, a spectacle that put Rossetti off public exhibition of his work. Championed and supported by John Ruskin, it was often through the great critic that Rossetti found a market. In the early 1850s, the artist and poet Elizabeth Siddal became his lover and favourite model, often cast as characters from Dante. Rossetti delayed marrying Siddal until 1860, when she was already gravely ill. When Siddal died in 1862, Rossetti buried the only complete manuscript of his poems with her (he had them exhumed seven years later). A flamboyant and recognisable figure – the archetypal bohemian – Rossetti was sought out by younger artists, among them Edward Burne-Jones and William Morris, with whom he formed a second generation of the PRB. After Siddal's death, Rossetti moved to 16 Cheyne Walk, which he shared with a menagerie including deer, exotic birds and his beloved wombat, Top, whose own death inspired the improbable verse tribute: 'Neither from owl nor from bat/ Can peace be gained until I clasp my wombat.'

# NOTTING HILL AND HOLLAND PARK

## INSTITUTIONS

### 18 STAFFORD TERRACE
18 Stafford Terrace, W8 7BH
rbkc.gov.uk/subsites/museums.aspx

The home of *Punch* cartoonist and illustrator Edward Linley Sambourne, preserved decorated as it had been in the late nineteenth century. Includes Sambourne's enormous collection of early photography, as well as his own original drawings.

### LEIGHTON HOUSE
12 Holland Park Road, W14 8LZ
rbkc.gov.uk/subsites/museums.aspx

The nineteenth-century studio home of Frederic, Lord Leighton is one of London's most extraordinary buildings, its ornately tiled lower rooms a Victorian fantasia of Islamic decorative traditions. The collection includes oil paintings and sketches by Leighton, casts of some of his significant sculptures, hundreds of drawings and works on paper, and related works by artists in Leighton's circle. Ticketed.

### THE MOSAIC ROOMS
Tower House, 226 Cromwell Road,
SW5 0SW
mosaicrooms.org

Non-profit space dedicated to contemporary culture from the Arab world; exhibition gallery, bookshop, film screenings and talks. The site of debut solo shows for the great Syrian-born painter Marwan and film-maker Basma Alsharif.

## COMMERCIAL GALLERIES

### PIANO NOBILE
96/129 Portland Road, W11 4LW
piano-nobile.com

Long-established gallery with roots in Italy, and a taste for old and modern masters. Twentieth-century British painting dominates the exhibition program in Holland Park; there's also a concept space at Kings Place in King's Cross.

# LUCIAN FREUD

Doggedly unsentimental toward his sitters – be they lovers, children or friends – Freud painted from prolonged observation from life. On moving studio to Holland Park in the late 1970s, he spent three years studying one corner to acclimatise to the light, resulting in an intense study of tangled vegetation: *Two Plants* (1977-80). The plants had it easy: sitting for Freud was an elongated affair, extending to months and even years to include time for background elements which the artist insisted on painting with the human subject in situ. As a result, his sitters are often marked with an air of melancholy introspection, their vividly rendered flesh settling into slack mounds and valleys. The grandson of Sigmund Freud, he was born in Berlin in 1922 and moved to Britain with his family in 1933. Art studies at Central and Goldsmiths colleges were fitted around a stint in the Merchant Navy between 1941-2. By the late 1940s he had developed a finely painted and precise linear style dominated already by pale flesh tones, cool lighting and spare interior detail. In the late 1950s he started using hogs-hair brushes and much thicker paint, which often amassed on the finished canvas. The piles of rags on which he cleaned brushes regularly appeared in later work, as did his beloved whippet Pluto. He was an artist celebrity by the 1990s, occasionally condescending to paint the famous, among them Jerry Hall (pregnant, naked) and The Queen (clothed, crown-wearing). The most important models of his later career were performance artist Leigh Bowery, Sue Tilley (aka 'Big Sue,' then working as a cashier at Bowery's nightclub Taboo) and his studio assistant David Dawson. Bowery stands apart among Freud's sitters in refusing to allow his face to relax, apparently entering into a battle of wills with the process of portraiture. Tilley appears in some of Freud's most celebrated late works, including *Benefits Supervisor Sleeping* (1995). 'Sometimes he was very chatty, sometimes he was very quiet – I always thought he should have been on the telly,' she told *The Guardian*. 'He'd say terrible things about people, but he never saw that he was really rude. I was always a bit jealous: he did exactly as he pleased. He was funny, miserable, horrible, kind, mean, generous, every character trait mixed up in one person.' It is Dawson and his whippet Eli who appear in Freud's final, unfinished portrait, made in 2011.

# HAMMERSMITH AND WEST KENSINGTON

## INSTITUTIONS

**ELEPHANT WEST**
62 Wood Lane, W12 7RH
elephant.art/west/

Not the unfortunately named offspring of Kanye West and Kim Kardashian, actually a hip-yet-approachable art space opened under the banner of *Elephant* magazine. Occupying an old petrol station forecourt, the gallery has an in-house bar, and street-food-van-turned-lunch-station, with space to hang out amid the art. Free.

**UNIT 1**
1 Bard Road, W10 6TP
unit1gallery-workshop.com

Gallery with a studio residency program founded by artist Stacie McCormick in a former builders' merchant's yard. Unit 1 is about giving artists and curators time to think and space to play with. Exhibitions from the three annual residencies are interspersed with shows by guest curators. Free.

## COMMERCIAL GALLERIES

**333**
333 Portobello Road, W10 5SA
hotshoemagazine.com

Modest photographic gallery within a café and bookshop run by the highly regarded photography magazine *HOTSHOE*, whose offices share the address.

**DAVID HILL GALLERY**
345 Ladbroke Grove, W10 6HA
davidhillgallery.net

Dedicated photography gallery largely showing unseen work by known and not-so-known twentieth-century photographers, including Bill Bernstein, Sanlé Sory, S.J. 'Kitty' Moodley and Billy Name. Works in concert with neighbouring Serena Morton.

**FRESTONIAN**
2 Olaf Street, W11 4BE
frestoniangallery.com

Named in honour of local squatters' attempts in 1977 to establish the Free and Independent Republic of Frestonia rather than accept eviction. The red brick People's Hall now occupied by the gallery was once the focal point of the Frestonia protest movement. On show: works from the twentieth century as well as recent painting and sculpture.

**SERENA MORTON**
343 Ladbroke Grove, W10 6HA
serenamorton.com

Popular local gallery with a tendency to bold painting and print works, run by prolific former pop-up gallerist Morton.

# EALING AND CHISWICK

## INSTITUTIONS

**CHISWICK HOUSE**
Burlington Lane, W4 2RP
chiswickhouseandgardens.org.uk

Neo-Palladian dwelling built in the 1720s by Richard Boyle, 3rd Earl of Burlington. Burlington was, in a phrase now sadly lapsed from fashion, a 'gentleman architect' as well as a great patron and collector. William Kent designed (and painted) much of the interior, and much of Burlington's collection remains in situ, including works by Murillo and Mytens, and views of the grounds by Pieter Andreas Rysbrack. Ticketed.

**HOGARTH'S HOUSE**
Great West Road, W4 2QN
williamhogarthtrust.org.uk

Hogarth's home in town, from 1733, was on Leicester Fields (now Leicester Square). The house in Chiswick was purchased in 1749. 'The most interesting house in Chiswick is Hogarth's,' wrote Arthur St John Adcock in *Famous Houses and Literary Shrines of London* (1897). 'It is a red brick villa in the Queen Anne style, with a quaint, over-hanging bay window, and stands in a large walled garden, not far from the parish church.' Hogarth called it his 'villakin' and had a studio at the foot of the garden. The house has suffered damage from neglect, fire and a parachute mine; the interior is a reconstruction, hung with prints of his etchings. Free.

## PITZHANGER MANOR
Mattock Lane, W5 5EQ
pitzhanger.org.uk

Country residence of Sir John Soane; the architect used to walk here from his house on Lincoln's Inn Fields at dawn, catch a fish in the pond, then take a carriage back to town to start his working day. The building has just been restored, with an adjacent art gallery for contemporary art; they opened with an exhibition by Anish Kapoor. Ticketed.

## SYON HOUSE
Syon Park, Brentford, TW8 8JF
syonpark.co.uk

London home of the Duke and Duchess of Northumberland; grounds designed by Lancelot 'Capability' Brown and much of the house reconstructed by Robert Adam between 1750-70. Art-wise, there's a tendency to barely clad statuary in the Greek and Roman style. The Red Drawing Room has a spectacular ceiling painted by Cipriani, and there are family portraits dating back to the mid sixteenth century. Ticketed.

Work by Anish Kapoor in the gallery at Pitzhanger Manor

# PETER BLAKE

Will Peter Blake ever transcend the collage he created for The Beatles' *Sgt. Pepper's Lonely Hearts Club Band*? Certainly for those growing up in the 1970s and 80s, his work was all around without our realising it. His famous picture of a (fictional) female wrestler, *Babe Rainbow* (1968), was printed on tin in an edition of 10,000: one of the many affordably priced multiples he produced in a long career. Paintings by Blake's Brotherhood of Ruralists adorned the editions of Shakespeare used in schools and colleges in the 1980s. One of the most celebrated of the British pop artists, Blake graduated from the Royal College of Art in 1956. Besides his ready embrace of screen-printing and other methods that made his work accessible to a broad audience, Blake broadcasts his interest in popular culture and consumer goods through paintings such as *Self Portrait with Badges* (1961), in which he appears dressed in branded American clothing clasping a record by Elvis. Blake has remained prolific, recently experimenting with different forms of printmaking. An enthusiastic collector – largely of craft objects and folk art, from shell-covered boxes to carnival signage – parts of his hoard have also been exhibited in their own right.

# GUSTAV METZGER AND AUTO-DESTRUCTIVE ART

One of the original signatories to Bertrand Russell's anti-war group, The Committee of 100, Metzger was committed to radical politics and non-violent protest. His first experiment with auto-destructive art was part of an anti-nuclear protest in 1959: he painted acid onto nylon so that it rapidly shrivelled and consumed itself. In 1960 he undertook his first *Public Demonstration of Auto-Destructive Art* at Temple Gallery (then in the basement of 8 Sloane Street), introducing his ideas on auto-destructive art 'as a desperate last-minute subversive political weapon...an attack on the capitalist system... (an attack also on art dealers and collectors who manipulate modern art for profit).' Born in Nuremberg in 1926, Metzger came to England in 1939 as part of the Kindertransport. 'Facing up to the Nazis and the powers of the Nazi state coloured my life as an artist,' he told *The Guardian* in 2012. 'When I saw the Nazis march, I saw machine-like people and the power of the Nazi state...Auto-destructive art is to do with rejecting power.'

TAIN

TIVE

N

OGH

BRITAIN

LICO

LETTERS

90 - 98

EAST

# SHOREDITCH AND SPITALFIELDS

## INSTITUTIONS

**AUTOGRAPH**
Rivington Place, EC2A 3BA
autograph.org.uk

Founded in 1988 as the Brixton-based Autograph, the Association of Black Photographers, this gallery on Rivington Place is only the most visible aspect of a hard-working organisation with an incredible history and the archive to show for it. The gallery is responsible for a diverse and stimulating program, consciously pushing the interpretation of photography to its limits, with exhibitions, such as Zanele Muholi's astonishing *Somnyama Ngonyama, Hail The Dark Lioness,* touring other venues. Free.

**FILET**
103 Murray Grove, N1 7QP
filetfilet.uk

Experimental project space in the studio of artists Uta Kögelsberger and Rut Blees Luxemburg. Run by artists, for artists, this studio show space is open for previews and by appointment.

**PEER**
97-99 Hoxton Street, N1 6QL
peeruk.org

Independent shopfront gallery immersed in the local community. They've hosted great projects here over the last 20 years, including exhibitions by Danh Võ, Mike Nelson, Fiona Banner and Emma Hart. Look out for the pedestal clock by Chris Ofili on the corner. Free.

**STANDPOINT**
45 Coronet Street, Hoxton, N1 6HD
standpointlondon.co.uk

This artist-run gallery and studios is one of the rare London spaces to invite artists to submit exhibition proposals. The aim is to support new work and ideas, showing work chosen from open submissions interspersed with exhibition concepts developed by the artist team. Free.

**TURNING EARTH**
Railway Arches 361-362,
Whiston Road, E2 8BW
AND
11 Argall Avenue, E10 7QE
turningearth.uk

Cult ceramics studio popular with artists. Hosts regular selling exhibitions.

(Previous pages: Sclater Street, Shoreditch)

# COMMERCIAL GALLERIES

## BLUE PROJECTS: BLUE MOUNTAIN SCHOOL
9 Chance Street, E2 7JB
AND
28 Old Nichol Street, E2 7HR
bluemountain.school

'Concept store' sounds dreadfully early-noughties, but in a very elevated way that's what Blue Mountain School is: a townhouse radically renovated by 6a architects, home to a VERY exclusive restaurant, 'open archive' clothing shop, perfumery and rare consumables. Blue Projects is their exhibition arm, and it's a class act.

## DELPHIAN
Various locations
delphiangallery.com

Young nomadic gallery staging pop-up shows around Shoreditch. It's early days, but so far the inclination is toward painting and photography that translates well into editions. Delphian also invite submissions to an annual open-call show.

## EMALIN
Unit 4 Huntingdon Estate
Bethnal Green Rd, E1 6JU
emalin.co.uk

This young gallery in a scrappy little space has been punching well above its weight with presentations of art from the new east: the poignant film works of Aslan Gaisumov, a fantastic archaeological museum constructed by Evgeny Antufiev, and a sauna installed during Frieze week by Augustas Serapinas.

## HALES
7 Bethnal Green Road, E1 6LA
halesgallery.com

Gallery with roots in Deptford (in the early 1990s) and a branch in New York (as of 2018). They're interested in shining a light on the recent past, as well as the ultra-new, showing historic work by Gladys Nilsson, Frank Bowling and the late Carolee Schneemann, and photographic works from the 1970s by Sunil Gupta.

## HOUSE OF AFRICAN ART
Various locations
houseofafricanart.com

New gallery representing contemporary artists (largely painters) from Africa and the African diaspora.

# TRACEY EMIN

Emin has become totemic of the bumptious rise of the East London art scene in the early 1990s. Never shy of the spotlight, her work mines harrowing biographical details that at times made it hard to judge where the woman ends and the work began. For the early video *How It Feels* (1996), the artist narrated her experience of a botched abortion, in which the patriarchal medical establishment's failure to take her concerns seriously almost led to her death. Her notorious *My Bed* (1998) is a self-portrait in absentia – the tormented sheets of an unmade bed surrounded by empty vodka bottles and other debris indicating the catastrophic experience of heartbreak. The appliquéd fabric tent *Everyone I Have Ever Slept With 1963–1995* was included in Sensation, an exhibition of recent works drawn from Charles Saatchi's art collection at the Royal Academy. With Emin's profile soaring, the work was wilfully misread by the media as a list of the artist's sexual conquests (in fact, the names were of those she had shared beds with since childhood, including her grandmother and unborn children). Long before the dawn of #MeToo, Emin has openly and frankly addressed her experience of rape, and its cultural normalisation in her hometown of Margate. She dealt in female suffering at the sensitised and bloody end, far from the conventional subject matter favoured by the (still male-dominated) artworld, where rape, if it appeared, was the prettified and dramatised stuff of classical myth. Early trauma continues to inform her work, but just as she shared the unexpurgated experience of being a young woman, so she has engaged frankly with the complications of growing older: recent paintings have explored the twin grief of her mother's death and Emin's realisation that she will never have children herself. She has also exhibited a series of photographic self-portraits documenting her insomnia, and which show her recovering from surgery around the eyes. Now, as then, her territory is that of messy emotion and the inconvenient, unpoetic response to real life.

## KATE MACGARRY
27 Old Nichol Street, E2 7HR
katemacgarry.com

Calm, understated gallery whose lovely list of mid-career artists include Goshka Macuga, Rana Begum, Peter Liversidge and Francis Upritchard.

## L'ÉTRANGÈRE
44a Charlotte Road, EC2A 3PD
letrangere.net

The Camus-inspired title identifies a gallery interested in the sensation of moving through life like a stranger; sensitive, in other words, to the rapid changes in contemporary society. The gallery has strong ties to the contemporary Polish scene, and often stages thematic exhibitions exploring ideas such as the environment or the domestic sphere.

# PUBLIC ART

## MUSTAFA HULUSI POSTERS

Hulusi started poster-bombing his own work around East London about 20 years ago. In 2017 he started hosting monthly single-poster residencies for other artists in a street-front frame at 2 Hoxton Street.

# ARTANGEL

Driven by a belief that the best and most exciting place for art is beyond the stultifying confines of a gallery, over the last 30 years Artangel have supported ambitious site-specific projects by artists in weird and unexpected locations. Most have taken place in London (some, such as Jeremy Deller's *Battle of Orgreave*, necessarily have not), punctuating the capital's everyday with moments of extraordinary, often fabulous oddness. Recently, Miranda July opened up a multi-faith charity shop in the fashion department of Selfridges, and Taryn Simon brought professional mourners from across the world to perform haunting laments in a subterranean amphitheatre in Islington. Artangel made both Michael Landy's *Break Down* (2001) and Rachel Whiteread's *House* (1993) possible, and have parlayed the use of spaces as sublime as the Palace of Westminster and as sombre as Reading Prison. Not every project is site specific: some are merely logistically mind-blowing. During the 2018/19 academic year, with the support of Artangel, artist and film director Steve McQueen photographed every Year 3 class in London for an exhibition at Tate Britain.

Hales Gallery, Shoreditch

# A FÊTE WORSE THAN DEATH

A Fête Worse Than Death was a village fair YBA-style, organised around the junction of Rivington Street and Charlotte Road, home to the favoured Barley Mow and Bricklayer's Arms pubs, and to Joshua Compston's Factual Nonsense gallery. Compston was the originator of the Fête, which opened on 31 July 1993 featuring Tracey Emin as a fortune teller, a Whack-the-Rat stall run by Gavin Turk, and Adam Chodzko's pubic hair exchange. Damien Hirst and Angus Fairhurst dressed as clowns and sold spin paintings made using a squeezy bottle of paint and a record player. 'A spin painting bought at the fete cost £1 and was signed by both artists on the reverse,' explains curator Gregor Muir in his memoir *Lucky Kunst* (2009). 'For an extra 50p the artists would reveal their spot-painted bollocks, an elaboration on the part of their make-up artist for the day, Leigh Bowery.'

# GILBERT & GEORGE

'I hope very much that you won't succeed,' the sculptor Anthony Caro is said to have told his pupils Gilbert & George. 'But I rather think you might.' It was 1968, and G&G were explaining their new approach to art – together, as a living sculpture – to those they thought might help. 'None of our teachers wanted to know us. Most encouraging!' the duo later told their friend and biographer Daniel Farson. At the time they sported their twinned initials and likenesses pasted to their foreheads, and proposed various improbable public works to London's councils and museums, with no success. Robert Fraser gave them a break, and they showed their 'magazine sculpture' *George the Cunt & Gilbert the Shit* (1969) – photographs of the duo grinning in the sunshine with the titular words collaged to their chests – in his Mayfair gallery. The neat suits they wore have become a trademark. So, too, the disconcerting clash between their respectable appearance and the interest in bodily functions, dirty talk and sexual invitation, broadcast by their stained-glass-window-like multi-panel photo works. G&G (born Gilbert Prousch and George Passmore) are a London institution, still beautifully dressed, impeccably polite and residents, since 1968, of Fournier Street.

# BETHNAL GREEN AND MILE END

## INSTITUTIONS

### AUTO ITALIA
44 Bonner Road, E2 9JS
autoitaliasoutheast.org

Artist-run organisation commissioning and producing new work, but also investigating and discussing recent cultural histories. Recent shows have included a survey exhibition of AIDS activist art collective Gran Fury, and screenings of radical artist sex films from the 1960s and 70s. Free.

### CELL PROJECT SPACE
258 Cambridge Heath Road, E2 9DA
cellprojects.org

Started in 1999 as an artist-run space, Cell now run seven buildings of artist studios, as well as this project space which hosts exhibitions, screenings and events led by invited artists. Free.

### CHISENHALE GALLERY
64 Chisenhale Road, E3 5QZ
chisenhale.org.uk

One of London's legendary, career-making art spaces. Don't even try coming on an opening night; the queue goes down the block. Come any other time and you'll see why: emerging artists are given carte blanche, with their ideas explored and documented in a free exhibition leaflet. Founded in the early 1980s, decade on decade Chisenhale have given debut UK solo shows to defining artists of their time, from Rachel Whiteread to Hito Steyerl. Free.

### V&A MUSEUM OF CHILDHOOD
Cambridge Heath Road, E2 9PA
vam.ac.uk/moc

Admittedly, there aren't many art galleries that offer Pirate Camp among their activities, but children's art is still art, whether it's made by, for or about children. Permanently installed on site is Rachel Whiteread's *Place (Village)* (2006-2008), assembled from the artist's collection of doll's houses. Collection free, exhibitions ticketed.

# JOHN AKOMFRAH
## and the Black Audio Film Collective

A standout commission for the 2015 Venice Biennale, John Akomfrah's audio-visual triptych *Vertigo Sea* went on to tour Britain. Distressingly prescient, the work explored the ocean as a site of migration and death. Using original and archive footage it linked the fates of the thousands of migrants then crossing the Mediterranean from North Africa, with that of civilians dumped from helicopters into the deep sea by General Pinochet's regime in Chile, enslaved Africans cast overboard on the Middle Passage, and the sea creatures eulogised in Heathcote Williams's epic poem *Whale Nation*. Shows at the prestigious Lisson Gallery followed, as did many more commissions for epic film installations – notably the post-war environmental disaster movie *Purple*, installed in the Barbican's Curve gallery in 2017. Such recognition was not before time. Born in Accra, Ghana, in 1957, Akomfrah was a co-founder of the Black Audio Film Collective, established by undergraduates in Portsmouth in 1982, and working out of Dalston between 1983 and 1998. Over 16 years, the collective were responsible for experimental and resolutely internationalist works that occupied territory between art, film and television. Their award-winning debut film *Handsworth Songs* (1986) was made in response to civil disturbances in Birmingham and London. Since 1997, Collective members Lina Gopaul and David Lawson have worked with Akomfrah as Smoking Dogs Films, making broadcast documentaries as well experimental works for exhibition. In 2018, Akomfrah's *Mimesis: African Soldier* was one of the concluding works commissioned by 14-18 NOW, commemorating the First World War and those who died in it. *Mimesis* honoured the African and colonial participants in the war: soldiers, and the millions who died labouring as porters, carriers and auxiliaries.

Chisenhale, Mile End

Maureen Paley, Bethnal Green; work by Gardar Eide Einarsson

Herald Street, Bethnal Green

4Cose, Bethnal Green

# COMMERCIAL GALLERIES

### 4COSE
7 Vyner Street, E2 9DG
4cose.co.uk

One of the few places in London you can find both art and really good parmesan. 4COSE is a shop and sometimes gallery space at the front of artist duo Cullinan Richards's studio. 4COSE means 'four things', about as many products as they tend to keep in stock.

### ANNKA KULTYS
Unit 3, First Floor
472 Hackney Road, E2 9EQ
annkakultys.com

Focussing largely on multimedia art and work often confined to digital platforms, Kultys programs her space to present six solo shows a year, as well as group exhibitions showcasing young graduates and guest curators.

### THE APPROACH
47 Approach Road, E2 9LY
theapproachtavern.co.uk

Why aren't more galleries located above a pub? The Approach has everything you need for a perfect Saturday afternoon: two little galleries showing interesting work upstairs; beer, veggie burgers and real fires downstairs. Bliss.

### CAMPOLI PRESTI
223 Cambridge Heath Road, E2 0EL
campolipresti.com

This Paris-based gallery works with a gorgeous list of artists, including painter Amy Sillman, collective fictional entity Reena Spaulings and conceptual (but sometimes also commercial) photographer Roe Ethridge. The result is shows with all kinds going on beneath the surface. Pay attention!

### HERALD STREET
2 Herald Street, E2 6JT
heraldst.com

This unassuming space is one of two run by Herald Street (the other being in Bloomsbury). It may not look like much, but they work with some fantastically irreverent and attention-grabbing artists, much in demand for institutional shows.

### IMT
Unit 2/210 Cambridge Heath Road
E2 9NQ
imagemusictext.com

Aka Image Music Text, an intermedia/new media/multimedia art space that represents artists (including contemporary miniaturist Paola Ciarska) but also hosts

## MAUREEN PALEY
21 Herald Street, E2 6JT
maureenpaley.com

The Queen of Bethnal Green, New York-born Paley first started showing in East London as Interim Art in 1984, a gallery that had 'legendary status,' according to curator Gregor Muir. In his YBA autobiography *Lucky Kunst,* Muir explains that, in the 1990s, 'Paley occupied a dominant position in the minds of young artists.' Paley changed the name on the gallery's twentieth anniversary, and still works with an incredible list of artists, including Wolfgang Tillmans, Gillian Wearing and Rebecca Warren.

## MODERN ART
50-58 Vyner Street, E2 9DQ
AND
4-8 Helmet Row, EC1V 3QJ
modernart.net

Modern Art's double-storey main space has big, high-ceilinged galleries perfect for showing large works of sculpture. The upper floor is sometimes used more like a project space.

Project Native Informant, Bethnal Green

# YINKA SHONIBARE CBE

Shonibare's work is synonymous with Dutch Wax: patterned cloth derived from Javanese Batik, first produced by the Dutch in the nineteenth century and largely sold to West Africa. Representing a microcosm of colonial appropriation and exploitation, the cloth also raises questions about authenticity, and suggests identity as a kind of performance. 'My work comments on power, or the deconstruction of power, and I tend to use notions of excess as a way to represent that power – deconstructing things within that,' the artist said in an interview with *BOMB* Magazine in 2005. Shonibare has used the cotton cloth for elaborate period costumes for film and photographic tableaux, and to dress sculptural works often featuring mannequins in Victorian dress. The ruffled and corseted costumes familiar from historical dramas look jarring in brightly patterned cloth, suggesting how absent other aspects of the colonial story are from prevailing narratives of Britain's past. In 2010, Shonibare created a model of Nelson's ship inside a giant glass bottle – its sails in Dutch Wax cloth – for the Fourth Plinth of Trafalgar Square. It now stands outside the National Maritime Museum in Greenwich. For an artist whose work explores the long tail of Britain's imperial past, the irony of being awarded Member of the 'Most Excellent Order of the British Empire' (MBE) was inescapable; Shonibare elected to add the title to his professional name. He has since been appointed a Royal Academician and awarded the CBE.

# RACHEL WHITEREAD AND *HOUSE*

In 1993, with the support of the commissioning body Artangel, Rachel Whiteread cast the inside of a three-storey house slated for demolition at 193 Grove Road. For a few years already, Whiteread had been making sculptural casts of negative spaces – the interior of a hot-water bottle, the undersides of furniture items – and in 1990 had shown *Ghost* at the nearby Chisenhale Gallery. *Ghost* was the cast of a room from a Victorian terraced house in Islington, much like the one Whiteread had grown up in; a three-dimensional evocation of a space full of memories that you could no longer enter. The construction of *House* was complex, requiring a team of builders and engineers to secure the concrete sculpture before the façade of the original building was destroyed around it. *House* immediately attracted controversy, and Whiteread found herself caught up in a cultural and political storm in which the sculpture became a rallying point in debates about housing, poverty and regeneration. On the same night that Whiteread was awarded the Turner Prize for the work, she also learned that the local council – many of whom were vociferously opposed to the sculpture – had passed a vote to have it demolished.

# THE SHOP

In 1993, friends Sarah Lucas and Tracey Emin – aka 'The Birds' – took a six-month lease on a former doctors surgery at 103 Bethnal Green Road, opening it as a studio/gallery/performance called The Shop. While it never made more than beer money, the shop sold knowing trinkets made by the pair in situ, including mobiles, badges, and ashtrays with Damien Hirst's face at the bottom. Open all night on Saturdays, The Shop became a hangout, placing the two artists at the centre of a scene celebrating a rough, DIY type of making. 'What's your best seller?' asked Gregor Muir, in a Q&A for *Frieze* magazine. 'Sarah Lucas: Ummm... The Rothko comfort blankets sell quite well, so do the little "Rescue Me" labels and our bestselling T-shirt is "Complete Arsehole". All the T-shirts are hand-painted and go up in price every time we sell one. They start off at £12, go up to £15 and then they go up in fivers until they get up to fifty pounds. What happens after that, we haven't decided. But "Complete Arsehole" is now selling at £40. Tracey Emin: And then the next expensive one is £35 and that's "Fucking Useless".'

## MOTHER'S TANKSTATION
58-64 Three Colts Lane
Bethnal Green, E2 6GP
motherstankstation.com

Where most galleries are founded on a vague idea, mother's tankstation has a manifesto, and one that quotes Shakespeare and Arthur C. Danto, at that. ('The *body of work*, as best manifested in the "gallery/museum shows", remains the purest truth of both an artist's intent and a gallery's purpose', apparently.) The mother tankstation, if you will, is in Dublin – its London spawn shares the same terrific list of up-and-comers, among them Yuri Pattison, Mairead O'hEocha and Lee Kit.

## PROJECT NATIVE INFORMANT
58-64 Three Colts Lane, E2 6GP
projectnativeinformant.com

PNI embrace oddness in a very good way. The work they favour is often disconcerting, playing, in its presentation, with the language of advertising, anthropology or fashion, and often, in its concerns, with questions of cultural identity. Artists include Harumi Yamaguchi, Sophia Al-Maria, DIS, Juliana Huxtable and Hal Fischer.

## ROMAN ROAD
69 Roman Road, E2 0QN
romanroad.com

Small double-height space in a shopfront gallery. They've shown some interesting work, including pioneering Polish feminist video artist Natalia LL.

## THE RYDER PROJECTS
19a Herald Street, E2 6JT
theryderprojects.com

Founded by Barcelona-born one-time art advisor Patricia Lara, Ryder has its sights set far beyond Bethnal Green. Her artists are freewheeling when it comes to media, and they even stage performance, using the industrial shutter at the front of the tiny project space as a curtain for an audience positioned out on the street.

## SOFT OPENING
4 Herald Street, E2 6JS
AND
Piccadilly Circus underground station
softopening.london

The gallery that started as a shopfront in Piccadilly Circus tube station now also has a space you can step into. Programming-wise, curator Antonia Marsh follows her fancy.

# CHANTAL JOFFE

*Personal Feeling is the Main Thing*, ran the title to Joffe's recent solo exhibition. Well, quite. Feeling is unmistakeable in Joffe's paintings: her figures assert a decided attitude, which suggests, in turn, a complex relationship between them and the artist, even (or perhaps especially) when she is painting herself. 'I think portraiture or the painting of people is always an act of trying to do the impossible – imaging your way into somebody else,' she says. Fascinated by the instability of the figure as seen, Joffe is drawn to bodies undergoing transformation: adolescents, new born babies, pregnant women. As with her close friend Ishbel Myserscough, Joffe studies her own changing body and face, often in relation to that of her daughter, exploring the complex, contradictory feelings bound up in motherhood. 'As we grow sexually invisible to almost everybody else, I want to make us visible because we're here and we matter,' she says of painting middle-aged women. 'We're smart and we're interesting and we're beautiful.' For her public artwork at the Crossrail station at Whitechapel, she drew on years spent observing her fellow Londoners on public transport, creating a set of portraits in paper collage, or what she calls 'drawing with scissors.'

# WHITECHAPEL

## INSTITUTIONS

### WHITECHAPEL GALLERY
77-82 Whitechapel High St
Shadwell, E1 7QX
whitechapelgallery.org

Leaving aside Whitechapel's storied history for a moment (it's been arting up the East End since 1901), let's bow down to curator Iwona Blazwick, who's programming has seen the gallery become a trailblazer for near gender equality. (On average, 40% of Whitechapel's shows are by female artists, by comparison to 22% at the Hayward Gallery, and 16% at Centre Pompidou, according to a 2015 study.) There's usually one big, ticketed exhibition, and a number of free displays and artist projects.

Whitechapel Gallery; Is This Tomorrow? exhibition (2019)

# THE WHITECHAPEL BOYS

In the early twentieth century a quarter of the population of London's East End was Jewish, immigrants who fled persecution in Central and Eastern Europe. Yiddish, poverty and Modernist inclinations bound a group – among them artists David Bomberg, Jacob Epstein, Mark Gertler, Jacob Kramer, Bernard Meninsky, Clara Birnberg and Alfred Wolmark – known as the Whitechapel Boys. 'They were not a manifesto group, though many of them were friends, fellow walkers who welcomed their neighbourhood gallery as a site in which to promote their own undoubted genius,' Iain Sinclair wrote of them. Through the Jewish Education Aid Society they studied at the Slade School. Sinclair suggests they found themselves, if not excluded, then actively patronised by their peers. In 1914, Bomberg selected works for a Jewish section in Whitechapel Gallery's grand survey exhibition, Twentieth Century Art: A Review of Modern Movements. The following year, a Jewish arts society named after biblical craftsman Bezalel Ben Uri was founded in Gradel's restaurant in Whitechapel. While the Whitechapel Boys (and girl) did not focus exclusively on East End subjects, paintings such as Bomberg's *Ghetto Theatre* (1920) and Mark Gertler's *The Rabbi And His Grandchild* (1913) offer glimpses of the London of their childhood.

# RICHARD HAMILTON

*Just what is it that makes today's homes so different, so appealing?* asked Richard Hamilton's 1956 collage, used as the poster for the exhibition This is Tomorrow, at Whitechapel. Constructed using images drawn from advertising, the collage showed a body builder and glamour model positioned within an ideal home dressed with the latest innovations in communications technology – he, brandishing an outsized lollypop, she reclining coyly beside a tin of ham. It evokes an image culture of pure consumerism, in which masquerade and real life were already becoming hard to separate. Hamilton's 'pop' vision embraced Picasso and Elvis alike, the world of television and the world of Marcel Duchamp. (Hamilton reconstructed Duchamp's *The Bride Stripped Bare by Her Bachelors, Even* in 1966 while teaching at the University of Newcastle; it subsequently furnished his student of the time, Bryan Ferry, with an album title.) Hamilton embraced commercial media: screen-printing in the 1960s, and ink-jet in the 1990s. He also continued to paint, producing, in the 1980s, a celebrated series of diptychs relating to the 'troubles' in Northern Ireland: *The citizen* shows a Republican detainee at the Maze prison; *The subject*, a parading Orangeman; *The state*, a British soldier on patrol.

# COMMERCIAL GALLERIES

## CARLOS/ISHIKAWA
Unit 4, 88 Mile End Road, E1 4UN
carlosishikawa.com

Vanessa Carlos is one of London's young art powerhouses; she is the founder of Condo, the global gallery-hosting initiative. Lodged in the back corner of an unprepossessing yard off Mile End Road, this still feels like a young gallery, but their artists are really bringing it. A recent video installation by Korakrit Arunanondchoi went straight from Mile End to the Venice Biennale.

## GALLERY 46
46 Ashfield Street, E1 2AJ
gallery46.co.uk

Unconventional space in two Georgian houses in the grounds of Whitechapel Hospital, staging shows that dance around the borders of graphic art, fashion and the margins of popular culture, as well as invited shows by students and emerging artists.

## GAO
Unit 7, 88 Mile End Road, E1 4UN
gao.gallery

Not the U.S. Government Accountability Office; actually a gallery…

## UNION PACIFIC
17 Goulston Street, E1 7TP
unionpacific.co.uk

Not North America's premier rail franchise; actually a gallery …run by two project-space veterans who made the move from Peckham. Artists to love on their list include Zadie Xa, for her gorgeously costumed, quasi-mystical performance works, and Urara Tsuchiya, for making ceramics REALLY sexy (and throwing pandas and anteaters into the mix).

## YAMAMOTO KEIKO ROCHAIX
19 Goulston Street, E1 7TP
yamamotokeiko.com

A gallery with a roving and unconventional eye. Recent shows included a sprawling solo by English Romani artist Delaine Le Bas, featuring sculpture, painting and embroidery and celebrating the life of the artist's late husband, activist-artist Damian Le Bas. Not your usual white cube fodder.

# DOCKLANDS

## INSTITUTIONS

**AREBYTE**
Java House, 7 Botanic Square
London City Island, E14 0LG
arebyte.com

Arebyte's exhibition program is supported by rent raised from studio complexes across London, and the whole enterprise is infused with a community sensibility. Exhibitions tend to be digital and new media in focus (think virtual and augmented reality, CGI and their digital brethren) and often loop in guest curators and emerging talents brought up through Arebyte's artist incubator. Naturally, there is also an online exhibition platform.

## FREEZE

Opening in the former Port of London Authority building on 7 August 1988, Freeze was the first in a series of warehouse exhibitions organised by a circle of Goldsmiths College students loosely clustered around Damien Hirst. Hirst used his considerable power of persuasion to raise money for a catalogue and materials, as well as the space. The 16 young artists – including Mat Collishaw, Michael Landy, Angela Bulloch and Anya Gallaccio – expended huge energy to make the space workable, as well as installing their artworks. It marked a turning point, with artists focusing on showing – professionalising, for better or worse – not just making. 'For Freeze, Damien Hirst got hold of some gallery mailing lists, which isn't a hard thing to do, it's just not something a lot of students would have thought of then,' recalls artist and critic Matthew Collings in *Blimey!* (1997). 'Consequently quite illustrious art people, like Norman Rosenthal from the Royal Academy and Nicholas Serota from the Tate Gallery, and some collectors, and some curators and critics and private gallerists… all came to the exhibition.' Freeze unrolled in three parts; it was in the third that Hirst showed the first of his spot paintings, emerging from his role as gobby organiser into that of artist.

# ANISH KAPOOR

A leading figure in what was known as the New British Sculpture scene in the 1980s, Anish Kapoor's floor and wall-based works at that time were often flooded with pure pigment. Those intensely matt, powdery surfaces created the appearance of deep voids in the sculptures' hollows, and suggested a certain immateriality to the forms, as if they could be blown away with a sneeze. In 1990, he represented Britain at the Venice Biennale, and the following year won the Turner Prize. Still exploring ideas of depth and solidity, his work led him to stone and steel, often creating sculpture that used a combination of shadow and pigment to suggested an incalculable void. Born in Bombay in 1954, Kapoor started out studying electrical engineering in Israel, before moving to London in 1973 to study at art school. You can see a bit of the engineer in his work: his interest in structure and pushing materials to their limits. Since the mid 1990s, he has worked with highly polished stainless steel, creating reflective works that present a vision of the world with proportions altered. Among these is the massive *Cloud Gate* (aka The Bean) installed in Chicago in 2006. Kapoor's concave reflective discs, the *Sky Mirrors*, have also been presented as temporary public artworks in Nottingham, New York and London. His most visible public sculpture in London, commissioned to coincide with the Olympic Games, is also something of an anomaly. The swirling, gridded steel tower of the *ArcelorMittal Orbit* doesn't fit neatly into his sculptural vocabulary – even less so since one of artist Carsten Höller's swirly metal slides was added to it a couple of years ago. Apparently as a kind of psychic counterbalance to all that mirror-polished perfection, Kapoor has a parallel interest in mess and disgust: in 2006, he started working with sticky red wax, creating moving works that left marks and smears on the gallery space. More recently he has used red silicone, both as a painting medium and as a surface coating to sculptural works.

# HACKNEY

## INSTITUTIONS

### BANNER REPEATER
**Platform 1, Hackney Downs Network Rail
Dalston Lane, E8 1LA**
bannerrepeater.org

People in the artworld overuse the term 'platform', but the artist-run reading room, project space and, er, artist book platform Banner Repeater is on an actual platform, in Hackney Downs station. They house Publish and Be Damned's public library, host reading groups and distribute free artist posters and pamphlets. No ticket required.

### GUEST PROJECTS
**Sunbury House, 1 Andrews Road, E8 4QL**
guestprojects.com

The guest in question is an invited artist (or dancer, musician, writer…) given a free studio space for a month by Yinka Shonibare CBE, to use as an experimental playground. The Project space's occasional supper club, the Artist Dining Room, allows guests to commune with an artist through the medium of food. Previous editions have included dinners dedicated to the great spiritual abstractionist Hilma Af Klint and surrealist artist and writer Leonora Carrington.

## COMMERCIAL SPACES

### LUNGLEY
**Haggerston Pub, 438 Kingsland Road
E8 4AA**
lungleygallery.com

Spirited shows in the cellar of local pub, The Haggerston. Zealous installations make virtue of the limited space.

### NEW ART PROJECTS
**6D Sheep Lane, E8 4QS**
newartprojects.com

Substantial subterranean space near London Fields run by artist-turned-gallerist Fred Mann. The tight list of emerging and mid-career artists is strong on drawing and painting, but there's also space for more conceptual work. Mann frequently invites other curators in for shows with artists from outside the gallery, which keeps things spicy.

# JO SPENCE AND THE HACKNEY FLASHERS

Jo Spence played many roles in her short career. Starting as a high-street studio photographer, Spence became fascinated by the politics of the photographic image: the power dynamic between photographer and subject, and the automatic adoption of socially ascribed personae for the camera. She was also interested in the world that was not shown: the authentic self, life unperformed, women's work. Spence was co-founder of the Hackney Flashers, a group active from 1974 until the early 1980s which brought attention to women's unpaid domestic labour and their struggle to keep going in a borough where little provision was made for their support. Spence often worked collaboratively – with partner Terry Dennett, and Rosy Martin – in series that wittily re-drew the power dynamic between photographer and subject. In 1982, she was diagnosed with breast cancer, and used photography to explore the dehumanised way her diseased body was seen by the medical profession, and the defeminising that accompanied mastectomy. Eight years later she contracted leukaemia. In *The Final Project* Spence pictures herself facing death: poetically, merging with the earth; with black humour, amassing grim deathmask trinkets for Halloween displays; and honestly, in the devastating final portraits from her hospital bed.

# HOUSE OF BEAUTY AND CULTURE

The avant-garde boutique, design studio and crafts collective House of Beauty and Culture sold one-off objects collaged from urban detritus – postal sacks, broken chairs, metal machine parts – informed by the DIY spirit of the punk era its members had grown up in. Founded by shoe designer John Moore in the shop space beneath his home at 34-6 Stamford Road, HOBAC was open for three years from 1986, and stocked jewellery by Judy Blame, fashion by Christopher Nemeth and Richard Torry, and furniture by Frick + Frack, and was documented for the fashion press of the day by photographer Mark Lebon.

## ROCKET
4-6 Sheep Lane, E8 4QS
rocketgallery.com

Founder Jonathan Stephenson has been making and designing books since he was a teenager. The gallery emerged from Stephenson's supremely collectible Rocket Press and reflects its founder's taste for bold graphics, strong colours and form, working with photographer Martin Parr, designer Imi Knoebel and painter Michelle Grabner.

## SEVENTEEN
270-276 Kingsland Road, E8 4DG
seventeengallery.com

Director David Hoyland has a formidable reputation as a talent-spotter, specifically when it comes to artists working in video and new media: he's held early career exhibitions by Jon Rafman, Oliver Laric and Marianna Simnett. Shows are reliably slick and irreverent: a recent exhibition by David Raymond Conroy involved the artist attempting to sublet the gallery as a durational artwork.

## SPACE STUDIOS
129-131 Mare Street, E8 3RH
spacestudios.org.uk

This great organisation providing artists with work spaces was co-founded by Bridget Riley in 1968 and now runs some 20 artist studio complexes across the city. Their Mare Street studios also have an exhibition space, in which artists are invited to consider the Hackney context they're operating in.

# PUBLIC ART

## HACKNEY MOSAIC PROJECT
Hackney Downs Pavilion,
Downs Park Road
Clapton, E5 8NP
AND
Shepherdess Walk, Hoxton
Hackney, N1
hackney-mosaic.co.uk

If you spot a gorgeous new mosaic in Hackney, it's likely the work of artist Tessa Hunkin, who has been sharing her skills with local residents with addiction and mental health problems since 2012. Together they've made sizeable designs for sites including Shepherdess Walk Park and Hackney Downs.

# WALTHAMSTOW

## INSTITUTIONS

**WILLIAM MORRIS GALLERY**
Lloyd Park, Forest Road
Walthamstow, E17 4PP
wmgallery.org.uk

The great designer lived in this Georgian house with his mother and eight siblings in his teens and early twenties. Inside, there are displays on Morris and his work, and exhibitions that relate in spirit to the man and his ideas about art and society. Ticketed.

## WILLIAM MORRIS

Artist, designer, poet, novelist and revolutionary socialist, William Morris approached life at a whip-crack pace and achieved extraordinary things. Part of the second wave – with Edward Burne-Jones – of the Pre-Raphaelite Brotherhood, he formed the firm eventually called Morris & Co in 1861. Like the PRB, Morris & Co. was founded on an appreciation of early art and poetry, close observation from nature, and the spiritual importance of beauty. Morris believed that industrial production broke the human spirit, separating head, hand and heart; instead, the skilled maker should be honoured by creating each design start to finish, an ethos at the heart of the subsequent Arts & Crafts movement. Morris taught himself to weave, and created enduringly popular designs for textiles and wallpaper from stylised plant forms. His later years were increasingly dedicated to political work, travelling tirelessly to address workers' groups. Access to art was essential to his vision, as Morris wrote in *Hopes and Fears for Art* (1882): 'I believe that art has such sympathy with cheerful freedom, open-heartedness and reality, so much she sickens under selfishness and luxury…I do not want art for a few, any more than education for a few, or freedom for a few.'

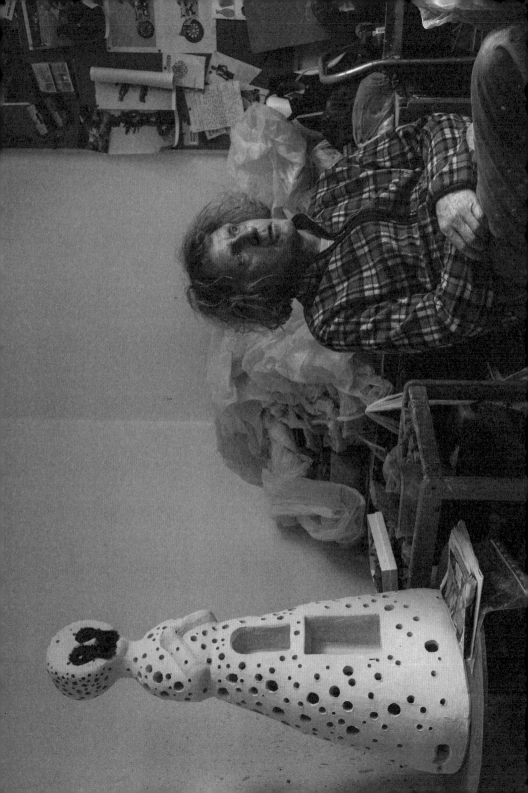

# GRAYSON PERRY
## and The Walthamstow Tapestry

Perry's political pots won him the Turner Prize in 2003, but his TV explorations of the subjects that fuel his work – gender, national identity, class and taste – have made him a celebrity. That and his magnificently dressed female alter ego Claire, a stalwart of the fashionable society columns. Perry well understands the power of appearances and the expectations that image carry. He uses benign forms with homely craft associations – vases, tapestries, clothes – to smuggle in discomforting critique. Lest we forget that he still works hard as an artist, a show of newish works – titled *The Most Popular Art Exhibition Ever!* – recently toured the UK. Fifteen metres long, *The Walthamstow Tapestry* (2009) presents the human lifecycle as experienced in contemporary London, with its protagonists passing from birth to death surrounded by clusters of brand names. Every developmental stage is repackaged as an opportunity for consumption: from Pampers and Glaxo Smith Kline attendant at their birth, to Marks & Spencer and the BBC accompanying middle age, and worthy causes siphoning off their lifeblood on their demise. 'It's almost like a religious fresco celebrating obscure gods and beliefs,' Perry told *The Guardian* at the time. 'I hope it ends up in the foyer of a bank.'

SOUTH

# SOUTHWARK

## INSTITUTIONS

### AFRICA CENTRE
Arch 28, Old Union Yard Archives
229 Union Street, SE1 0LR
africacentre.org.uk

Opened in 1964 as a cultural hub for London's diasporic populations, the Africa Centre's mixed cultural program has included several important exhibitions, among them the touring Open Exhibition of Black Art, organised by the Blk Art Group (Eddie Chambers, Keith Piper, Claudette Johnson and Donald Rodney) in 1982, as well as an eponymous Blk Art Group exhibition in 1984. In 1983, Lubaina Himid staged Five Black Women, showing her works alongside Sonia Boyce, Claudette Johnson, Houria Niati and Veronica Ryan. The Centre moved from its historic home in Covent Garden in 2013: a gallery at its new Southwark site is set to open soon. Free.

### HAYWARD GALLERY
Southbank Centre
Belvedere Road, SE1 8XX
southbankcentre.co.uk

The South Bank's famous Brutalist gallery got a loving facelift just ahead of its fiftieth birthday in 2018, and it's brighter and lighter within as a result. Working closely with artists, and often taking advantage of the massive ceiling height and huge walls, the Hayward has hosted many memorable shows, including solo outings for Henri Matisse, Richard Long, Anish Kapoor, Bridget Riley and Jeremy Deller. Ticketed.

### JERWOOD PROJECT SPACE
171 Union Street, Bankside, SE1 0LN
jerwoodarts.org

Exhibition space belonging to the leading independent funding body on the UK arts scene. Jerwood supports earlyish-career artists at transitional moments; a great place to discover upcoming talents. Free.

### SCIENCE GALLERY
Great Maze Pond, SE1 9GU
london.sciencegallery.com

This new gallery, attached to King's College, loops together ideas from science, art and medicine to bring multiple perspectives to pressing themes, from understanding addiction to the future of food. Free.

(Previous pages: Dulwich Picture Gallery)

Hayward Gallery, Southbank Centre

**TATE MODERN**
Bankside, SE1 9TG
tate.org.uk

Colossal gallery in the former Bankside Power Station and a twisted pyramid erected alongside it, dedicated to modern and contemporary art of increasingly international flavour. Three galleries for ticketed exhibitions run alongside free collection displays and live performances. Expect a bewildering array of talks, events, screenings and education programs. A prestigious annual commission occupies the Turbine Hall between October and April: previous editions have included Olafur Eliasson's misty sunset, an ocean of handmade porcelain sunflower seeds installed by Ai Weiwei, and an interactive performance by Tino Sehgal.

**VO CURATIONS**
Twelfth Floor, 11 York Road, SE1 7NX
vocurations.com

Gallery and studio complex incongruously located on the twelfth floor of an office block, run by a cosmopolitan artist and curatorial team that divides its activities between London and Paris.

# THE OTHER STORY

In 1989, the Hayward Gallery was the site of a radical exhibition organised by artist and writer Rasheed Araeen. The Other Story offered a vision of modern Britain as reflected by artists of Asian, African and Caribbean origin: a gesture by way of antidote to decades in which these artists had found their work cordoned off from the dominant narrative of art history. This was not only the other story of modern British art, but also the story of 'othering' in modern British art. 'It is not a story of so-called "black art" or "ethnic minority arts". The Other Story is a recognition of Afro-Asian contributions to post-war British Art,' the exhibition text explained. 'It is the constant preoccupation of the dominant culture to look for cultural differences in the work of those artists who are neither European nor white. This may be an innocent fascination with the exotic but underlying it is a complex problem within Modernism which excludes the Other from its centre.' Araeen's selection ranged from the older generation, including Ronald Moody and F.N. Souza, through the foaming sculptures of David Medalla, through to emerging artists of the new generation, among them the prodigiously talented Sonia Boyce, whose work *Big Women's Talk* (1984) appeared on the exhibition's poster.

# R.B. KITAJ AND THE SCHOOL OF LONDON

The US American-born artist R.B. Kitaj studied alongside David Hockney at the Royal College of Art in the late 1950s. After 15 years teaching in California, he returned to London in 1972, and was invited by the Arts Council to buy works for a themed show of British art from the period. The result, in 1976, was The Human Clay, an exhibition of (gasp) figurative drawing and painting, staged in a period dominated by minimalism and conceptualism. 'This odd old, put upon, very singular place,' Kitaj wrote of London in his catalogue essay. 'Each one of you who reads this conducts his or her own very complex affair with London and yet how often does our art look as if it had been made here? Dickens and T.S. Eliot knew this place and how I wish for a London art that would body forth at those levels of quality.' Thus he proposed the existence of an emerged School of London, among its number Lucian Freud, Francis Bacon, Michael Andrews, David Hockney (then, in point of fact, resident in California), Frank Auerbach, Howard Hodgkin and Leon Kossoff. Figurative painters all, it is otherwise a diverse group, but the term has stubbornly endured.

# BOMBERG AND THE BOROUGH GROUP

David Bomberg – constantly innovating, usually rebelling, barely selling and routinely rejected in his attempts to wring a living from art – led anti-establishment evening classes at Borough Polytechnic between 1945 and his move to Spain in 1953. 'It is impossible at this distance to convey just how big a potential danger to orthodoxy Bomberg's classes were in the parochial climate prevailing in the art schools of London in the years just after the Second World War,' wrote one of his students, artist Roy Oxlade, years later. 'Inevitably Bomberg's influence at the Borough Polytechnic was seen as threatening. Students from other London art schools attending his part time and evening classes were seen, and saw themselves, as subversives.' Among the Bomberg subversives were: Frank Auerbach, Leon Kossoff, Dorothy Mead, Miles Richmond and Cliff Holden. Groups of them exhibited together as the Borough Group, and later as the Borough Bottega.

# DEREK JARMAN AND ANDREW LOGAN AT BUTLER'S WHARF

In the 1960s and 70s, before yuppie developments sanitised the abandoned Thames-side warehouses of London's south bank, the derelict spaces were a haven for artists needing cheap space. The ad hoc (often squatted) complexes housed studios, exhibitions, happenings, parties and homes for those who could cope with sub-zero temperatures. Film-maker and artist Derek Jarman was resident in various buildings between 1968 and 79, often in neighbouring studios with performance artist Andrew Logan and his brother, the sculptor Peter Logan, and the painter Tony Fry. Jarman filmed the fire ritual for *In the Shadow of the Sun* – which featured Andrew Logan, and was soundtracked by Throbbing Gristle – on the waste ground near Butler's Wharf, and returned to the area for parts of *Jubilee* (1978) and *The Last of England* (1987). Logan held his third 'pansexual beauty pageant' Alternative Miss World at Butler's Wharf in 1975. Notable participants included Jarman as Miss Crêpe Suzette, John Maybury as Miss Windscale Nuclear Power Station and Grayson Perry as Miss St Claire Perry of Essex.

# GREENWICH

## INSTITUTIONS

### NOW GALLERY
The Gateway Pavilions
Peninsula Square
Greenwich Peninsula, SE10 0SQ
nowgallery.co.uk

Glass-fronted gallery hosting three annual commissions by figures from across the creative sphere – among them fashion designers Phoebe English, Charles Jeffrey and Molly Goddard – yielding dramatic installations. Free.

### QUEEN'S HOUSE GREENWICH
Romney Road, Greenwich, SE10 9NF
rmg.co.uk

Designed in 1616 by Inigo Jones for King James I's wife, Anne of Denmark, purportedly as an apology for swearing in front of her after she killed one of his favourite dogs while hunting. Now part of the National Maritime Museum, it houses great artworks on a nautical theme, including the 'Armada Portrait' of Elizabeth I, works by J.M.W. Turner,

Joshua Reynolds and William Hogarth, and Canaletto's handsome painting of the House itself. The ceiling of the great hall is a contemporary work by Turner Prize winner Richard Wright. Ticketed.

## RANGER'S HOUSE
Chesterfield Walk, SE10 8QX
english-heritage.org.uk

Georgian villa on the border of Greenwich and Blackheath, home to the Wernher Collection (though not to the German-born Sir Julius Wernher himself, who gathered the 700 artworks and antiquities with a fortune accumulated from his management of South African gold and diamond mines). Highlights include works from the Italian and Northern Renaissances, and medieval statuary. Ticketed.

# PUBLIC ARTWORKS

## YINKA SHONIBARE CBE, *NELSON'S SHIP IN A BOTTLE* (2010)
Park Row, Greenwich Peninsula, London SE10 9NF

First commissioned for the Fourth Plinth in Trafalgar Square, Shonibare's giant bottle contains a detailed replica of HMS *Victory,* on which Nelson died during the Battle of Trafalgar in 1805. The ship is rigged with 37 sails stitched from Dutch Wax fabric, suggesting colonial trade routes and cycles of exploitation linked to Britain's maritime endeavours.

## ART ON THE GREENWICH PENINSULA
greenwichpeninsula.co.uk

Amid ardent development (15,000 new homes are on their way), there's been an ambitious program of public art commissioned for Greenwich Peninsula, including Alex Chinneck's nose-diving electricity pylon *A Bullet from a Shooting Star*; Conrad Shawcross's *Optic Cloak* (concealing the flue from the Peninsula's energy centre); and large sculptural works by Gary Hume, Antony Gormley and Richard Wilson. Most are long-term rather than permanent: check for updates.

# BERMONDSEY

# INSTITUTIONS

### ALMANAC
41 Acre Lane, SW2 5TN
almanacprojects.com

Small not-for-profit with spaces in London and Turin. Solo shows supplemented with reading groups, spoken word, screenings and performance. Free.

### BERMONDSEY PROJECT SPACE
183-185 Bermondsey Street, SE1 3UW
project-space.london

The interest here is in what happens when visual art hooks up with other creative media – dance, film, music – and even the sciences. A small project space over three floors of a converted Georgian paper factory with an intriguing, leftfield program, and a bustling events and education schedule. Free.

### MATT'S GALLERY
92 Webster Road, SE16 4DF
mattsgallery.org

Matt's Gallery (named after founder Robin Klassnik's dog) holds a unique position within London's art ecosystem, and the history of art in this city. Opened in 1979 in Klassnik's studio (then in Martello Street in the East End), Matt's prioritises the conception and creation of new work, offering artists space, time and support to explore ideas and methodologies. Highlights include Richard Wilson's *20:50* (1987), for which he filled the gallery with 200 gallons of used sump oil; Susan Hiller's disturbing four-screen Punch and Judy film *An Entertainment* (1990); and Mike Nelson's labyrinthine environment *Coral Reef* (2000). The gallery is due to move to a new site in Nine Elms during 2020, programming across both sites in the lead up.

### SOUTHWARK PARK GALLERIES
1 Park Approach
Southwark Park, SE16 2UA
southarkparkgalleries.org

Exhibition and residency spaces in Southwark Park run by the Bermondsey Artists' Group, responsible for joyous and dynamic contemporary commissions in all media. The white-cube gallery in the old Lido Café largely shows paintings, works on paper and video. Nearby Dilston

Southwark Park Galleries, Dilston Grove

Grove occupies the raw shell of an old church, one of the most atmospheric exhibition spaces in London: a site for sculpture, performance and experimentation. Free.

# COMMERCIAL GALLERIES

**SID MOTION**
24a Penarth Centre
Hatcham Road, SE15 1TR
sidmotiongallery.co.uk

Sid is one of the London art scene's young dynamos – she follows her passions, showing emerging artists of all ages (including one in their 60s and another still at art school), working largely in painting and photography. It's early days, but a recent move to this larger space betokens good things.

**WHITE CUBE**
144-152 Bermondsey Street, SE1 3TQ
OR
25-26 Mason's Yard, SW1Y 6BU
whitecube.com

This museum-sized second space for Jay Jopling's mighty London gallery oozes sinister, don't-mess-with-me power. It's housed some extraordinary shows over the last few years, including a lead-lined corridor set with metal hospital beds by Anselm Kiefer, a spirited historic exhibition of work by female surrealists, and a triumphant show of gut-wrenching new paintings by Tracey Emin.

Robin Klassnik, Matt's Gallery

White Cube, Bermondsey; Tracey Emin, *A Fortnight of Tears* (2019)

# VAUXHALL AND LAMBETH

## INSTITUTIONS

### BEACONSFIELD
Beaconsfield Gallery Vauxhall
22 Newport Street, SE11 6AY
beaconsfield.ltd.uk

An artist-run space occupying a former 'Ragged School', Beaconsfield hosts exhibitions, residencies and events: think of it as a grass-roots, socially engaged counterbalance to the slickness of nearby Newport Street (an artist-run space of a rather different kind).

### GARDEN MUSEUM
Lambeth Palace Road, SE1 7LB
gardenmuseum.org.uk

Founded near the site of the great botanical gardens created by the Tradescant family in the early seventeenth century, the Garden Museum has recently reopened after extensive renovation. Exhibitions of art on botanical themes, both trad and rad.

### GASWORKS
155 Vauxhall Street, SE11 5RH
gasworks.org.uk

Arts non-profit: the gallery being only the most visible manifestation of a long-respected residency and studio program drawing on Gasworks's formidable international network.

### IMPERIAL WAR MUSEUM, LONDON
Lambeth Road, SE1 6HZ
iwm.org.uk

Alongside more traditional conflict-related historical exhibitions, IWM has a dynamic track record for commissioning new works by contemporary artists. They're often REALLY good: Rosalind Nashashibi's *Electrical Gaza* saw her nominated for the 2017 Turner Prize; John Akomfrah's *Mimesis: African Soldier* was a highlight of 2018.

### MORLEY GALLERY
61 Westminster Bridge Road
South Bank, SE1 7HT
morleycollege.ac.uk

The gallery of Morley College hosts exhibitions by students and recent graduates, as well as emerging and established artists and designers. The college has a good art collection, including works by Edward Bawden, John Piper, Bridget Riley, Maggi Hambling and Denzil Forrester.

# SARAH LUCAS AT CITY RACING

Of the generation that graduated Goldsmiths College in the late 1980s and formed the core of the YBAs, Lucas has worked with remarkable consistency over three decades, producing sculpture in abject materials (tights, concrete, cigarettes) that explore conventions of sex and the gendered body. The British are weird about sex – uptight, prudish, obsessed, salacious, crude – and Lucas delights in teasing out our peculiarities. Early works such as *Two Fried Eggs and a Kebab* (1992), *Sod you Gits* (1990) – and her important early exhibition *Penis Nailed to a Board* (1991) at the artist-run City Racing gallery in Kennington – drew on the sexist, sex-obsessed culture of newspapers like the *Sunday Sport*. 'It's not that I think I'll put a load of sex in my work, it's just that that's what's sort of poking me in the eye,' she told Elizabeth Fullerton in *Artrage!* (2016). 'That stance of sitting on the fence about whether I liked it or not became part of what I was doing. I hate being told what to think anyway, so I'm certainly not going to be doing that myself.' Britain's crass underbelly has proved the basis for an eminent career: Lucas represented Britain at the Venice Biennale in 2015.

# THE TRADESCANTS' ARK

Eminent botanist father and son John (and John) Tradescant travelled widely – in Europe, Russia, the Americas and North Africa – in search of rare plant specimens with which they glorified the greatest gardens of England in the early seventeenth century. They gathered other things on their travels too, among them art, antiquities and natural history specimens. These were eventually displayed as a cabinet of curiosities in a building known as the Ark at their botanical garden in Lambeth. In 1638, beside the remains of curious and exotic fauna, the varied and uncategorised exhibits included 'a girdle such as the Turks wear in Jerusalem, the passion of Christ carved very daintily on a plumstone,' and 'the hand of a mermaid' according to the account of one visitor. Open to all for a small fee, this was Britain's first public museum, and the collection formed the basis of what is now the Ashmolean Museum in Oxford. There were reports of foul play involved in Elias Ashmole's acquisition of the collection from the younger Tradescant's widow: accusations involving theft, trespass, an ill-positioned dungheap and the wrongful sale of objects passed between the two, following which Hester Tradescant was found face down in a shallow pool, and Ashmole became custodian of the Ark and its contents. The Tradescant tomb still stands in the churchyard of St Mary at Lambeth, inspiring the founding of a Museum of Gardening History (now the GardenMuseum) in the dilapidated church building in 1977.

## NEWPORT STREET GALLERY

Newport Street, SE11 6AJ
newportstreetgallery.com

Damien Hirst, gallery proprietor? It should come as no surprise: Hirst's route to fame was due in no small part to his smarts as a curator, exhibition organiser, publicist and all-round showman. He's also a voracious collector of other artists' work. Newport Street Gallery opened in 2015 – a free, public space showing impeccably mounted exhibitions drawn from his collection, among them monographic shows on Jeff Koons, Gavin Turk and Ashley Bickerton. Hirst's support allows artists to realise works at a scale and quality not normally possible for public gallery exhibitions, and the artists love him for it.

# COMMERCIAL GALLERIES

## CABINET GALLERY

132 Tyers Street
Vauxhall Pleasure Gardens, SE11 5HS
cabinet.uk.com

Cabinet have managed to keep a grip on their too-cool-for-school status for over 25 years. Is it because they regard the artists, the gallery and all the subsidiary publishing and research activities as a collective enterprise? When they moved to their extraordinary new space on the site of the old Vauxhall Pleasure Gardens, artists including John Knight, Lucy McKenzie and Marc Camille Chaimowicz were invited to contribute to the design. Passion projects alternate with exhibitions by Cabinet's artists – among them Ed Atkins, Wu Tsang and Lily van der Stokker – though, in typically arch fashion, the gallery has been known to refer to art as 'Propaganda and Decoration'.

## SUNDAY PAINTER

117-119 South Lambeth Road, SE8 1XA
thesundaypainter.co.uk

You couldn't accuse the Sunday Painter of being risk averse – they've held some pretty out-there shows, including Rob Chavasse's video compilation of the gallery director's teenage skateboarding bloopers. The shows here are always interesting, working with artists including the great ceramic sculptor Emma Hart, and abstract painter Tyra Tingleff.

# DAMIEN HIRST

The figurehead of the YBA generation is now in his fifties, and presides over a vast studio-come-art-company (Science Ltd), an art collection (Murderme), publishing house (Other Criteria), public exhibition gallery (Newport Street) and restaurant (Pharmacy 2). Born in Bristol in 1965, and brought up in Leeds, Hirst moved to London in the mid-1980s and studied at Goldsmiths College. Many of his most significant techniques and preoccupations emerged during a furiously creative burst between the late 1980s and early 1990s: he showed his first spot paintings in the third part of Freeze, a sequence of professional-looking student exhibitions he masterminded in 1988, during his second year at college. Together with Carl Freedman and Billee Sellman, Hirst was also responsible for the shows Modern Medicine, Gambler and Market in the old Peek Freans biscuit factory in Bermondsey. In the first, Hirst showed *A Thousand Years* (1990). Twinned vitrines carried a fly hatchery, a severed cow's head and an Insect-o-cutor: flies would hatch, lay eggs in the head, then get zapped. Despite its putrid stench, it was purchased by Charles Saatchi for £4,400. The following year Saatchi lent Hirst funds to acquire a four-metre tiger shark, which was placed in a tank of formaldehyde as *The Physical Impossibility of Death in the Mind of Someone Living*. The same period also saw the first of Hirst's medicine cabinets and works with butterflies. During the 1990s, Hirst seemed to be everywhere: winning the Turner Prize in 1995, involved in The Pharmacy restaurant in Notting Hill, directing a pop video for Blur and even releasing a hit novelty record. Meanwhile, Hirst's collector base was becoming ever more international. In response, perhaps, to the control his gallerists exerted, on 15 and 16 September 2008, Hirst held an unprecedented two-day sale of new work at Sotheby's in London titled *Beautiful Inside My Head Forever*. The sale raised £111 million. It also coincided with the collapse of Lehman Brothers, heralding the start of a global financial crisis. Hirst spent much of the next decade masterminding a spectacular comeback – a practical joke on a grand scale staged at billionaire Francois Pinnault's private museums in Venice. *Treasures from the Wreck of the Unbelievable* purported to be a haul salvaged from the sea floor: in truth the 'coral'-encrusted marble and bronze sculptures, gold coins, weaponry, drawings and historic artefacts were all created by a vast team of specialist artisans under Hirst's direction. Controversial, as always, the show attracted international press coverage, and the crowds followed. The largest sculpture – the 16-metre *Demon with Bowl* (2014, inspired by William Blake's 1819 painting *The Ghost of a Flea*) – is now the centrepiece of the Kaos nightclub in Las Vegas.

# SUNIL GUPTA
## and 'Pretended' Family Relationships

'In the late 1980s a very interesting idea emerged in a roundabout way that lesbian and gay relationships were not real, or not as real as heterosexual relationships,' Gupta writes of 'Pretended' Family Relationships. The image and text series had started as a study of multi-racial gay couples in London – some real, some confected. The work took on new urgency in May 1988, with the Thatcher government's introduction of the notorious Clause 28, stating that no local authority should permit the promotion of homosexuality or 'promote the teaching of the acceptability of homosexuality as a pretended family relationship.' The final series was made up of triptychs, including an intimate portrait of a couple and poetry suggesting a private bond. Born in New Delhi, Gupta moved to Montréal as a teenager, then to London, for love, in his twenties. It was after the demise of this first major relationship, in 1984, that he made his studies of other gay couples in London: defying the cliché that homosexual relationships were fleeting and unstable, and defying, too, photography's dominant white, heterosexual viewpoint. A co-founder of the Association of Black Photographers (now Autograph ABP), Gupta also has an important legacy as a curator and educator.

# VAUXHALL PLEASURE GARDENS

Between 1661 and 1859 the Vauxhall Pleasure Gardens were London's foremost site of culture and entertainment in the summer months. Originally known as the Spring Garden, it was popular with Londoners escaping the bustle and filth on the opposite bank of the river, and famous for birdsong and sexual solicitation alike (Sir Roger de Coverley left one visit with the parting shot that 'if there were more nightingales and fewer strumpets' he might be a more regular visitor). In the 1730s, the Gardens were reimagined as a site of mass entertainment, where, for a small fee, all could enjoy concerts, exhibitions and illuminations within beautifully orchestrated views. Connections to the Prince of Wales were capitalised on: re-dubbed Vaux Hall, the Gardens became one of the most fashionable attractions of Georgian London, painted by Canaletto in 1751. Their golden period – associated with the music of George Frideric Handel and pictures of William Hogarth – lasted until around 1770. By 1784, when Thomas Rowlandson painted his watercolour *Vaux Hall*, the Gardens' reputation had once more become rather louche. With the new century came an escalation in entertainments, destined to lure back an ebbing crowd: balloon flights and acrobatic displays. As London expanded and new forms of popular entertainment flourished in the city, the gardens were sold off for development.

# WILLIAM BLAKE IN LAMBETH

London's great visionary poet, artist and prophet was born above a hosier's shop in Soho in November 1757. His home was an un-numbered building on the corner of Broad and Marshall Streets. Blake's parents were Dissenters, rejecting state religion: hence, perhaps, their decision to allow their son to escape schooling. Blake instead walked – from Soho, north up Tottenham Court Road toward Highgate and Harrow, or south, to Dulwich and Peckham Rye – building up knowledge of London that flooded through his later verse:

*The fields from Islington to Marybone,*
*To Primrose Hill and Saint John's Wood,*
*Were builded over with pillars of gold,*
*And there Jerusalem's pillars stood.*

Blake saw his first vision at Peckham Rye: aged eight or ten he looked up and discovered a tree filled with angels. Biographer Peter Ackroyd describes him as a 'Cockney visionary.' Visions – both of divine emanations and, later, of his dead family – accompanied his daily life. Blake showed an early aptitude for drawing and verse, and through the print shops around Soho he discovered the work of the Old Masters in black and white. He was sent to Henry Pars Drawing School on the Strand, and, at 15, apprenticed to the engraver James Basire of Great Queen Street, with whom he gained great proficiency. Although 'trade' was disapproved of in the rarefied Royal Academy Schools, Blake was accepted as a student in 1779 and formed an important friendship with sculptor John Flaxman. Following his marriage to Catherine Boucher in 1782, Blake developed the relief etching process with which he achieved his distinctive mingling of text and image: working on copper plates, he drew out his design in reverse in chalk, then painted over them in salad oil and candle grease, which resisted the acid solution in which the plate was treated, leaving text and image standing proud. Blake hand-coloured each plate before printing, bringing extraordinary intensity to his illuminated books. In 1790, he and Catherine moved to the Hercules Buildings in Lambeth, and it is here, over the following decade, that Blake created his greatest works, among them *Songs of Innocence and of Experience*, *The Marriage of Heaven and Hell*, *Visions of the Daughters of Albion* and the *Continental Prophecies*. Blake was certainly prone to eccentricities and unconventional behaviour, and was afforded little regard beyond the support of a few loyal patrons in his lifetime: for much of his life he struggled to balance the desire to immerse himself in his own compositions, and the need to fulfil commercial commissions to keep the household afloat. Blake died in 1872, working on illustrations to Dante's *Divine Comedy*: he is buried at the Dissenters' burial ground in Bunhill Fields.

# ELEPHANT AND CASTLE

## INSTITUTIONS

**DRAWING ROOM**
1-27 Rodney Place
Elephant and Castle, SE17 1PP
drawingroom.org.uk

Gallery, library and event hub dedicated to drawing, in all its traditional and experimental expressions. A great exhibition program is enlivened by talks, events and workshops. Look out for their fundraising Drawing Biennial. Free.

**PEAK ART**
Unit 340A, Ground Floor
Elephant and Castle Shopping Centre
SE1 6TE
peak-art.org

The sword of Damocles hangs over the terrazzo-floored Elephant and Castle Shopping Centre – and with it Peak Art, a project space and gallery occupying Unit 340A on the ground floor. Free.

**PLAZA PLAZA**
70 County Street, SE1 4AD
plazaplaza.co.uk

Shutter-fronted garage-space studio gallery founded by ceramic artist Jesse Wine in 2011. Open for exhibition previews and by appointment. Free.

**TURPS**
Unit 12, Taplow House, Thurlow Street
SE17 2UG
turpsgallery.co.uk

Lively studio program (and magazine) with a gallery attached, all dedicated to contemporary painting and painters. Free.

## COMMERCIAL GALLERIES

**GREENGRASSI / CORVI-MORA**
1a Kempsford Road, SE11 4NU
greengrassi.com
corvi-mora.com

Two galleries for the price of one, accessed through the same door. Greengrassi and Corvi-Mora share spaces through which they alternate shows: domestic-scaled upper rooms and garage-like white cube gallery at the back. Corvi-Mora's magnificent list includes painters Lynette Yiadom-Boakye and Jennifer Packer, and sculptor Roger Hiorns; Greengrassi's features Tomma Abts, Frances Stark and Lisa Yuskavage.

# CLAPHAM

## INSTITUTIONS

**STUDIO VOLTAIRE**
1a Nelsons Row, SW4 7JR
studiovoltaire.org

One of London's great non-profit spaces, Studio Voltaire is housed in a chapel-like space just off the high street. Clever and bold, Voltaire are unafraid to follow whims and passions in pursuit of interesting art with something to say. It's no exaggeration to say that others follow where they lead: whether it's championing the photography of Jo Spence or the sculpture of Phyllida Barlow, or hosting the astonishing Temple to Oscar Wilde by McDermott & McGough, the impact of their programming is felt across the UK and beyond. All that good work has not gone overlooked: they're expanding, requiring the gallery to close for a year from autumn 2019.

# MARIE SPARTALI STILLMAN

'"Always a model but never an artist" might well have served as the motto of the seriously aspiring young woman in the arts of the 19th century,' suggests Linda Nochlin in 'Why Have There Been No Great Women Artists?' A notable exception was Marie Spartali Stillman, who achieved a successful career on both sides of the Atlantic with luscious portrayals of (largely female) figures associated with dramatic poetry and myth. Spartali's father, the Greek Consul-General, was a patron of the arts and hosted garden parties in their home on Clapham Common. Thus Spartali came to the attention of the Pre-Raphaelite Brotherhood, who granted her the ultimate accolade of 'stunner'. Her likeness appears in works by Rossetti, Ford Madox Brown and Burne-Jones, as well as photographs by Julia Margaret Cameron. In 1864, she started studying under Madox Brown (as Rossetti had), and first showed work at the Royal Academy in 1870. The following year, she married the American art critic and writer William James Stillman. Writing being notoriously ill paid, it often fell to Spartali to help support their six children – which she did, working steadily, and regularly showing in Britain and the United States.

# BRIXTON

# INSTITUTIONS

## BLACK CULTURAL ARCHIVES
Windrush Square, Brixton, SW2 1EF
blackculturalarchives.org

Britain's great repository of Black history and culture. The building on Windrush Square houses a public archive, research facilities and social spaces as well as an exhibition gallery mounting historically important shows documenting aspects of Black British culture, from the 1980s music scene to the lives of Black Londoners during the Georgian period. Free.

## BLOCK 336
336 Brixton Road, SW9 7AA
block336.com

Large subterranean galleries attached to a studio complex, which lend themselves well to performance and live events and exhibitions by young and emerging artists. Free.

## BRIXTON UNDERGROUND STATION
Atlantic Road, Brixton

There's fresh art popping up all over the underground, but Brixton Station carries the crown, with a series of commissions inspired by the neighbouring murals created in the 1980s. Njideka Akunyili Crosby's magnificent *Remain, Thriving* (2018) was followed by Aliza Nisenbaum's group portrait of TFL staff, painted on site during a two-month residency. The next work in the series is by Denzil Forrester, known for his paintings of London's dub and reggae scene in the 1980s.

# PUBLIC ART

**BRIXTON MURALS**

There was a vogue for mural painting in 1970s and 80s London. By 1986, in the borough of Lambeth alone there were some 300 in public spaces, often along political themes. Development has done many of them in, but seven remain in Brixton, among them Brian Barnes and Dale McCrea's *Nuclear Dawn* (1981-1982) on Coldharbour Lane, which shows Death striding across London against a backdrop of distinctly psychedelic mushroom clouds, and Stephen Pusey's *Children At Play* (1981-82), commissioned in the aftermath of the 1981 riots. A map of the murals is available at Brixton underground station.

# ROTIMI FANI-KAYODE AND JAMES IN BRIXTON

For the six years of Rotimi Fani-Kayode's career he lived on Railton Road, Brixton's 'front line'. Here he staged photographs including the affectionate double portrait *Dennis Carney and Essex Hemphill in Brixton*. Fani-Kayode explored the male body: as a site of desire, a cultural object and, in the case of the Black male body, the subject of exploitation and myth. Bodies in his photographs occupy a complex universe that features Yoruba artefacts, stylised and apparently ritual behaviour, game play, BDSM, flirtation and tenderness. *James in Brixton* shows a young man with a metal eye patch; flipped and printed a second time, it becomes a kind of Yin Yang symbol. These two Jameses with their cropped bleached hair and their white shirt lying open offer an amused and inviting gaze that is anything but objectified. In his essay 'Traces of Ecstasy' (1982), Fani-Kayode addressed the exploitative mythologising of Black virility and described his personal experience of a kind of three-part otherness: as an African in Europe, as a gay man and as an artist, defying his parent's high society ambitions for him. A founder member of the Association of Black Photographers (now known as Autograph ABP) he died of AIDS-related complications in 1989.

# MONA HATOUM
## and *Roadworks*

In 1985, for a show of experimental art in public spaces, Mona Hatoum undertook an hour-long walk through Brixton barefoot with a pair of Doc Martens boots trailing from her ankles. Four years after the Brixton Riots, tensions still ran high. Doc Martens boots were associated both with the police and right-wing gangs: groups *Roadworks* suggested as inescapable and intertwined components of the systemic racism hampering her progress. Born in 1952 in Beirut, to a Palestinian family, Hatoum was stranded in London as war broke out in Lebanon in 1975. After studies at the Slade School, Hatoum worked first in performance and video, later with installation and sculpture, creating unsettling works exploring politics of the body, and the status of the individual in relation to geopolitical tension. *Light Sentence* (1992) – installed at Tate following Hatoum's nomination for the Turner Prize in 1995 – featured a stack of mesh cages around which a naked lightbulb moved on a track, casting oppressive shadows onto the walls of the gallery. Hatoum often works at the border of beauty and horror, weaving delicate structures in human hair, wiring electrical currents through domestic objects, or recasting deadly objects in seductive coloured glass.

# PECKHAM AND CAMBERWELL

## INSTITUTIONS

### ASSEMBLY POINT
49 Staffordshire Street, SE15 5TJ
assemblypoint.xyz

Artist-run exhibition space linked to a buzzy studio complex. Free.

### BOLD TENDENCIES
Seventh-Tenth Floors, Multi-Storey Car Park, 95a Rye Lane, SE15 4TG
boldtendencies.com

One of those initiatives that makes London feel like it might still be cool and youthful: 10 years ago, a group of young arty and foody types started staging summer shows on the roof of Peckham Car Park, complete with café and cocktail bar. The program has grown more sophisticated: recent commissions include works by artworld megastar Sterling Ruby, architectural interventions by sculptor Richard Wentworth and a bubblegum-pink staircase by Simon Whybray. There's an active community and education program and they've even hosted operas. Summer months only. Free.

### THE BOWER
'Ladies' Unit 1, Brunswick Park
Camberwell, SE5 7RH
thebower.org.uk

This small gallery in a converted public toilet block in Brunswick Park is funded by the nearby park café, which operates out of an old park keeper's hut. It's a ladies toilet, and uncoincidentally the exhibitions have all been by women artists. Directors Louisa Bailey and Joyce Cronin also run a publishing company on site. Free.

### FLAT TIME HOUSE
210 Bellenden Road, SE15 4BW
flattimeho.org.uk/

In 2003, John Latham declared his house a living work of sculpture and opened its doors to anyone interested in art. In 2008, two years after the artist's death, Flat Time House was re-opened in the same spirit, hosting events, artist residencies and exhibitions, many engaging with Latham's ideas and ideals. Free.

# JOHN LATHAM AND *ART & CULTURE*

In August 1966 John Latham withdrew Clement Greenberg's *Art and Culture* from the library of St Martin's School of Art. With a group of students, he removed and ate the pages of Greenberg's book, chewing the text to pulp then spitting it out. This spitty papier-mâché was left to ferment. Receiving an overdue notice from the library, Latham returned a vial that he explained contained the distilled 'essence' of *Art and Culture*. This vivid objection to Greenberg earned him a dismissal from his teaching post (though the work is now housed at MoMA in New York). Latham started using books as components in a body of work under the collective title 'Skoob' in 1958: they appeared jutting from painted canvases, sawed, pulverised or burned, the knowledge and words they contained rendered latent but inaccessible by their transformation. Latham also experimented with spray-painting, and with text and image works that unfurled on moving rollers, alongside written explorations of his theory of Flat Time. Damien Hirst wasn't the first to exhibit fish in a vitrine; Latham's *They're Learning Fast* (1988) featured a tank of live piranhas – the ultimate hostile public – circling four waterproofed pages from his text *Report of a Surveyor*.

# THE ARTIST PLACEMENT GROUP

Founded in the mid 1960s by Barbara Steveni, with John Latham, Barry Flanagan, David Hall, Anna Ridley and Jeffrey Shaw, the APG proposed artists as a resource. Rather than being kept remote from the public by a gallery system that rendered it untouchable, art should comingle with the worlds of industry, commerce and government, providing alternative perspectives and points of view: 'Context is half the work' was the group's guiding principle. APG organised placements for artists in which they would have carte blanche to research, propose and create art. During John Latham's own placement in the Scottish Development Office in 1975-6, he was invited to come up with a creative solution for dealing with heaps of coal waste, known as Bings. He suggested that they had an inherent monumental quality, and should remain in place, reimagined as a work of land art. Latham's personal philosophies informed much of the APG's discourse, and their negotiations with businesses were at times said to resemble works of performance art in their own right.

## SOUTH LONDON GALLERY
65-67 Peckham Road, SE5 8UH
southlondongallery.org

Looking for an institution that balances commitment to its local community with on-the-pulse international engagement? SLG is here to show you how it's done. They've been exhibiting art on this site for over 125 years, and SLG has gone through a recent period of expansion: it now extends to a back garden designed by artist Gabrielle Orozco, fancy new studios, and the once-derelict fire station opposite made gorgeous by 6a Architects. They stage fantastic shows here: Katharina Grosz spray-painted the inside of the old gallery to spectacular effect; Barbara Kruger has lined the interior with a text-y multimedia installation; Gilbert & George staged The Naked Shit Pictures; Superflex presented their film *Flooded McDonald's* and Michael Landy installed his *Art Bin*. SLG doesn't look to North London – it looks to the world.

South London Gallery; Haegue Yang, Tracing Movement exhibition (2019)

# JOHN RUSKIN

It is hard to know where to start, or indeed to stop, with Ruskin. To call him an art critic condemns him with faint praise – though an art critic he was, and an important champion of both J.M.W. Turner and the Pre-Raphaelite Brotherhood. Ruskin saw nature, art and society as intimately linked: the ideal of truth to nature is already at the heart of his 1843 defence of Turner, which forms the first volume of *Modern Painters*. The cossetted only son of a well-off family, Ruskin grew up in Herne Hill and travelled widely with his parents, first visiting Venice in 1835, aged 16. Ruskin studied at Oxford, and started collecting watercolours by Turner as a young man: *Modern Painters* commenced as a spirited defence of the artist against his critics. The PRB's commitment to the detailed painting of nature was inspired by Ruskin's writings; in turn, he wrote a letter to *The Times* in defence of Millais in 1851. Their lives became devastatingly intertwined: Ruskin's wife Effie annulled their unconsummated marriage and left him for Millais. Ruskin's writing extended to texts on the architecture of Venice, the Alpine landscape, drawing, Renaissance art, philosophy, social ideals, taste and morality, poetry, weather patterns, a work of fiction for young readers and the autobiography *Praeterita* (1885-89); even during his lifetime, reading groups were established dedicated to his works. In 1871 he founded the Ruskin School of Drawing and Fine Art at Oxford, but he also taught at the Working Men's College in London, and supported educational establishments for women. Ruskin formed the utopian Guild of St George in 1871, acquiring and parlaying land and artworks to give industrial workers access to beauty, and to encourage hand making. Ruskin's private life was catastrophic, thanks in no small part to the interference of his parents, and to his romantic fascination with young girls: details that have proved irresistible to modern biographers and screenwriters, often threatening to eclipse his legacy as a writer, educator and patron.

# COMMERCIAL GALLERIES

## BOSSE AND BAUM
Unit BGC, Bussey Building
133 Rye Lane, SE15 4ST
bosseandbaum.com

Great space in one of the units of the Bussey Building near Peckham Rye Station. They make a virtue of hosting artist performance and live events, but they also show painting and sculpture, including Emilie Taylor's distinctive ceramic works, painted screens by Luke Burton, and France-Lise McGurn's suggestively arranged painted figures.

## HANNAH BARRY
4 Holly Grove, Peckham, SE15 5DF
hannahbarry.com

Great little gallery, given to spirited exhibition installations. Barry is a local mover and shaker: co-founder of Bold Tendencies, the cultural non-profit that takes over rooftop spaces on the local car park during summer months.

## LILY BROOK
3 Ada Road, SE5 7RW
lily-brooke.com

This little gallery occupies the front room of curator Lily Brook's home, complete with fireplace and bay window out onto the street: details that add a distinctive flavour to shows in this small space.

# DULWICH

# INSTITUTIONS

## DULWICH PICTURE GALLERY
Gallery Road, Dulwich, SE21 7AD
dulwichpicturegallery.org.uk

In 1790, two London art dealers – Noël Desenfans and Francis Bourgeois – were charged with amassing a Royal Collection for Stanisław II Augustus, King of Poland. Over the following five years Desenfans and Bourgeois doggedly acquired works fit for a king. Following massive political upheaval in Poland, Stanislaw abdicated in 1795, leaving Desenfans and Bourgeois with a royal-less Royal Collection. The bulk of the collection was eventually left to Dulwich College boys' school. Sir John Soane's 1811 designs for Dulwich – which was to become Britain's first public art gallery – have had a huge influence on museum architecture through to the present day, in particular his use of natural light via glass lanterns in the ceilings. The collection – which includes fabulous works by Rembrandt, Van Dyck and Poussin – is shown alongside a program of temporary exhibitions, often of twentieth-century paintings.

## STEPHEN WRIGHT'S
## *HOUSE OF DREAMS*
**45 Melbourne Grove
East Dulwich, SE22 8RG
stephenwrightartist.com**

Textile designer Stephen Wright became so fascinated with the total environments created by 'outsider' artists that he decided to create his own: an exuberant House of Dreams packed with mosaic, panels of text, and textile and plastic sculptures that he's been working on for 20 years. Wright opens his house for one day a month. Ticketed, advance booking essential.

Dulwich Picture Gallery

# JEREMY DELLER'S
## Open Bedroom

In 1993, with his parents away on holiday, Jeremy Deller replaced the pictures in his family home with his own works, interspersed small art objects amongst the photographs and ornaments, and taped texts to the toilet walls. The resulting exhibition – Open Bedroom – was accessed by appointment. Deller was 27 and still living with his parents: this consciously anti-heroic exhibition was an acknowledgement of what the artist considered a rather embarrassing situation. It also fitted what were to become his abiding interests: art made outside the artworld from fan sketches to trade union banners; popular music; social participation; personal history as a microcosm of social shift. Most of Deller's work since has taken place outside of gallery situations, and much has required the participation of other people. In 2001, *The Battle of Orgreave* restaged a bloody clash between striking miners and the British police, using 800 specialist battle re-enactors as well as 200 former miners. There has been establishment recognition – he won the Turner Prize in 2004, and represented Britain at the Venice Biennale in 2013 – but Deller maintains a maverick streak. During the 2017 General Election, he was revealed as the anonymous creator behind posters reading 'Strong And Stable My Arse' that were pasted around London.

# WIMBLEDON

## INSTITUTIONS

**SCHOOL GALLERY**
Delta House Studios
Riverside Road, SW17 0BA
schoolgallery.co.uk

High-minded – if playful – gallery launched by artist and curator Michael Hall, who also runs the Invisible Print Studio producing artist editions. School stage four shows a year, issuing publications and running talks and events alongside. Free.

**WIMBLEDON ART STUDIOS**
10 Riverside Yard
SW17 0BB
wimbledonartstudios.co.uk

Artist studio complex hosting art fairs selling to the public in May and November.

## PAULINE BOTY

Pauline Boty's final painting *BUM* (1966) was commissioned by Kenneth Tynan for the erotic revue *Oh! Calcutta!* It shows a rounded posterior poking between theatre curtains underneath the royal crest. Bold, sexy and witty, it is the confident work of a young woman regarded as a leading light of British Pop Art. In 1961, just out of the Royal College, Boty exhibited alongside Peter Blake, and was one of four artists featured in Ken Russell's BBC documentary *Pop Goes the Easel* (1962). Known during her student years as 'the Wimbledon Bardot', Boty's striking appearance on screen attracted acting roles, among them a brief appearance in the film *Alfie*. Away from admiring casting directors, her painting and collage works became overtly political: *It's A Man's World I* (1964) pasted together patriarchal icons from Elvis to Einstein. *Countdown to Violence* shows a flag-draped coffin in front of portraits of John F. Kennedy and Abraham Lincoln, with a scene from the riots in Birmingham Alabama in the foreground. In 1965, Boty discovered that she was pregnant and had leukaemia – she died five months after giving birth, aged only 28. Largely written out of London's Pop Art story, her paintings were tracked to a barn on her brother's farm in 1993.

# DEPTFORD AND NEW CROSS

## INSTITUTIONS

**GOLDSMITHS CENTRE
FOR CONTEMPORARY ART**
St James's, New Cross, SE14 6AD
goldsmithscca.art

Can we start with the building? Assemble, the only architecture collective to win the Turner Prize, helmed the conversion of this Victorian bathhouse to eccentric but luscious results. Within, a dynamic curatorial team are bringing great contemporary art to Lewisham, interspersing large international shows with a quick-changing program of projects and displays that keeps the institutional finger on the experimental pulse.

## THE YBAS

At the turn of the 1990s, a generation of dynamic young artists making attention-grabbing work burst into the public sphere. Many were recent graduates from Goldsmiths College, among them Damien Hirst, Liam Gillick, Mat Collishaw, Angus Fairhurst, Abigail Lane, Angela Bulloch, Gary Hume, Anya Gallaccio, Michael Landy, Fiona Rae and Sarah Lucas, most of whom had studied under conceptual artist Michael Craig-Martin. Inspired by the new American art being shown at the Saatchi Collection on Boundary Road – and borrowing techniques from the world of advertising – they promoted their work through exhibitions in disused warehouse spaces. Saatchi took the bait, and by 1992 held the first of six Young British Art shows, 'sealing the label in the public consciousness to describe a diverse group of artists,' so writes Elizabeth Fullerton in *Artrage: The Story of the BritArt Revolution* (2016). 'For possibly the first time ever, a collector had created a movement.' The YBAs, as they soon became known, supplied the press with ample material for delighted outrage, whether in art – pickled sharks! Obscene child mannequins! Dirty jokes about eggs and kebabs! – or public behaviour. Indelibly associated with London during Tony Blair's 'Cool Britannia' era, the YBAs drew international attention to the city's art scene.

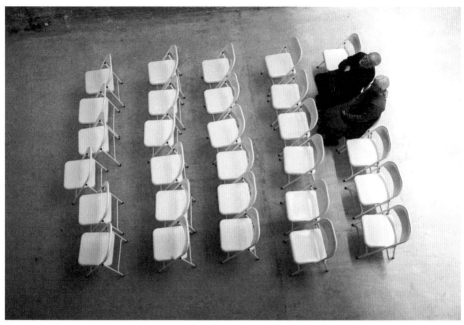

Goldsmiths Centre for Contemporary Art, New Cross

Caster Projects, Deptford; Lindsey Mendick, The Ex Files exhibition (2019)

# COMMERCIAL SPACES

**CASTOR PROJECTS**
Enclave 1, 50 Resolution Way, SE8 4AL
castorprojects.co.uk

This young gallery has recently risen to larger premises in Deptford, as well as a fully fledged commercial identity. They stage punchily installed exhibitions by a small roster of artists, some only recently graduated.

# BECKENHAM

# INSTITUTIONS

**BETHLEM MUSEUM OF THE MIND AND GALLERY**
Bethlem Royal Hospital,
Monks Orchard Road, BR3 3BX
museumofthemind.org.uk

Museum and gallery in the grounds of Bethlem Royal Hospital. This is the oldest psychiatric hospital in the world, and has been based at various sites around London over its 800-year history. Art and mental health are closely intertwined: the museum houses the hospital's archives and art collection, and stages fascinating exhibitions exploring themes from melancholy to mescaline. The gallery shows new work by artists who have experienced mental health issues.

# BATTERSEA

## INSTITUTIONS

**PUMP HOUSE GALLERY**
Battersea Park, SW11 4NJ
pumphousegallery.org.uk

Lively public gallery in the park, commissioning temporary public outdoor works as well as exhibitions.

## PUBLIC ART

**NICOLA HICKS,**
***BROWN DOG* (1985)**
Battersea Park, Battersea, London
SW11 4NJ

Hicks's dog replaces a memorial erected by anti-vivisectionists in 1906, commemorating a brown terrier allegedly subjected to illegal vivisection during a lecture at University College London in 1903. Emotively inscribed 'Men and women of England, how long shall these things be?', the memorial was routinely vandalised by medical students, and eventually placed under 24-hour guard. In 1907, the Brown Dog Riots saw medical students carrying effigies of the dog clash with suffragettes, anti-vivisectionists and the police. Media reports tended to side with the medical students: the contended canine was removed and melted down in 1910.

**HENRY MOORE,**
***THREE STANDING FIGURES* (1948)**
Battersea Park, Battersea, London
SW11 4NJ

Moore's draped stone figures, facing skywards, were shown in the first of a series of important Open-Air Sculpture Exhibitions held in Battersea Park between 1948 and 1966.

**BARBARA HEPWORTH,**
***SINGLE FORM* (1961-2)**
Battersea Park, Battersea, London
SW11 4NJ

Smaller version of the monumental bronze stationed outside the UN building in New York.

White Cube, Bermondsey

# INDEX OF PUBLIC ART

# INDEX OF VENUES

British Library Cataloguing-in-Publication Data
A catalogue record for this book is available from the British
Library

The author and publisher gratefully acknowledge the permission
granted to reproduce the copyright material in this book. Every
effort has been made to trace copyright holders and to obtain
their permission for the use of copyright material. The
publisher apologises for any errors or omissions in the text and would be
grateful if notified of any corrections that should be incorporated
in future reprints or editions of this book.

Design concept: Webb & Webb Design Ltd.

Front cover: Gillian Wearing with her sculpture of Millicent
Fawcett, Parliament Square
Back cover: Dulwich Picture Gallery
Frontispiece: Artists Chantal Joffe (left) and Ishbel Myerscough
Pages 4-5: Ishbel Myerscough's studio

Portions of the articles 'London's Vibrant Subcultures, Painted
Over Four Decades' and 'Stunningly Modern Paintings by a
Gender-Bending 1920s Artist' by Hettie Judah originally appeared
in The New York Times Style Magazine on January 25, 2017, and
February 1, 2017 respectively, are copyright The New York Times
and are used here by permission.

Acknowledgements
*Art London* is heavily indebted to the work of generations of
art historians; where appropriate, I have cited them in the text.
Thanks to Elizabeth Fullerton, Amah-Rose Abrams, Eddy Frankel,
Sam Talbot and Flan Flanagan, who have all checked sections of
the manuscript for screaming errors. To Andrew Whittaker of ACC
Art Books, who first proposed a book called Art London, and has
been a model of open-minded enthusiasm. To Alex Schneideman
for going above and beyond. To all the artists who sat for portraits
and to the galleries who helped make that possible. And to Ben,
Jacob and Isaac, for weathering the chaos.

MIX
Paper from
responsible sources
FSC® C124385
FSC
www.fsc.org

Printed in China
for ACC Art Books Ltd., Woodbridge, Suffolk, England

www.accartbooks.com

ACC
ART
BOOKS